I've had a ⟨...⟩ ⟨...⟩ and
it seems ve⟨...⟩
Happy Bir⟨...⟩
love Yuzo

NOTHING SO SIMPLE
AS CLIMBING

NOTHING SO SIMPLE AS CLIMBING

G. J. F. DUTTON

Illustrations by Albert Rusling

Diadem Books · London

Also by G. J. F. Dutton
The Ridiculous Mountains (Diadem Books, 1984)

Published in 1993 (in cased and tradepaper edition)
by Diadem Books, London

All trade enquiries to:
Hodder and Stoughton
Mill Road, Dunton Green, Sevenoaks, Kent TN13 2YA

Copyright © 1993 by G. J. F. Dutton

British Library Cataloguing in Publication Data
Dutton, G. J. F.
  Nothing So Simple as Climbing: More
  Adventures of the Doctor and His Friends
  in the Long-suffering Highlands
  I. Title
  823.914 [FS]

ISBN 0 906371 12 0 (cased)
ISBN 0 906371 17 1 (t/pb)

All rights reserved. No part of this publication may be
reproduced, stored in a retrieval system, or transmitted in any
form or by any other means, electronic, photocopying,
recording or otherwise without the permission of the publisher.

Printed and bound in Great Britain by
Biddles Ltd, Guildford and King's Lynn

CONTENTS

* First published in the *Scottish Mountaineering Club Journal* (between 1984-1993)
# First published in *One Step in the Clouds* (Diadem 1991)
§ First published in *Mountain* (130)

PREFACE

Those who have read the previous collection of Doctor stories will need no Preface. These few words are for the unprepared. As before, I myself am just a kind of Editor, having merely selected the tales below with the help of their Narrator. They recount his adventures among the hills with the (frequently) unhappy Apprentice and the (invariably) optimistic Doctor. The scene is usually the Highlands of Scotland, because that is where they mostly climb; and also because it is an area small enough to concentrate the reverberations of even a minor episode, and yet large enough to exhibit the awesome range of activities that now beset the enjoyment of mountains in any part of the world.

The characters accompanying – or afflicting – the Trio are familiar enough, whether from the previous volume or our own experiences, and their adventures no more fictitious than those described before; nor are the excuses put forward by mountaineers for indulging themselves any the less untrustworthy.

One participant more in evidence this time is the Doctor's wife, whose only contributions to the last volume were curtain material and the book's title. Regarding the latter, she has objected to the inference of considering mountains ridiculous. 'I have been misunderstood. You can't blame the hills. It's what you people do on them that is absurd. Such elaborate equipment, such endless argument. Surely quite unnecessary. After all, you only have to go up – to 3000 feet, or whatever it is – and come down. Why all the fuss? I should have thought there was nothing so simple as climbing....'

I have borne her remarks in mind when selecting the stories for this book.

BECAUSE WE WERE THERE

Our sport is frequently misunderstood. We are not socially irresponsible. We go out of our way to help others; if there is no alternative. Take one evening when the Doctor, the Apprentice and I were relaxing by the bar in the unlovely hamlet of Kilmoggie – that last hitch of the Industrial Belt – after a pretty hard day. The Apprentice had led three new E1s; and I had followed with drawn breath, adhering by the resultant suction. The Doctor, fresh from some meeting or other, was running us back. Not to be outdone, he tried a new route home, and got lost. We found ourselves in Kilmoggie and stopped at its single repellent hostelry for a belated celebration.

The Doctor was examining bottles for the next order when a boy's head poked round the door; stared at us; rotated, and howled ear-splittingly backwards: 'They're *here!*'

He approached, stepping over the sacks, rope and assorted gleamery which we uncharitably thought safer with us than in our car, whose boot would not lock that day.

'You climbers?'

We assented, with equal lack of grace; he appeared highly predatory.

He revolved once more; and shrieked: 'They're so: *climbers.*'

Then, to us, 'Come awa out.'

Mesmerised, we went out, the Doctor testily shaking his head and putting away spectacles.

Out there, a small group. Locals. A sort of delegation. A determined-looking wifie, well-endowed with shoulders and chest, disengaged herself and, accompanied by heads and eyes, marched up to us.

'You climb, eh?' We nodded. 'Then folly me.'

Ah, well; Fate had taken over. We followed. The rest fell in behind, muttering.

We turned down a small carboniferous lane. At the bottom, another crowd, larger. They parted, and we trailed through, the wifie striding in front. Then she halted and bellowed ahead:

'Here, Annie, I've brocht them Annie. Here's climbers for ya.'

Annie, an auld happit-aboot craitur five feet high and three feet away, raised keen – very keen – eyes to us. 'They'll help ye, Annie, they'll help ye.' All at ten decibels, for Annie was deaf; and then, fiercely, at ten and a half, to us: 'That right, eh?'

The Doctor summoned together all his professional bravura and replied briskly and with a dreadful gaiety, 'Of course, of course. Now,' bending towards Annie, 'What's the trouble?'

'I canna get it doon', she croaked, 'canna get it doon....'

The Doctor, with conclusions automatically oesophageal, laid a kindly hand on her shoulder. 'We'll have a look at it, then: let's go into your house.'

'Whit for ma hoose?' screeched Annie, eyes rounded, 'It's no 'n ma hoose!' The Amazon was more explicit. She grinned savagely. She smote the Doctor's shoulder. 'Up there, Chairlie, up there....' and raised her arm skyward. Reality was awaiting us.

Our gaze followed, and encountered a huge, a vast, tree. An ash of so straight and unhindered a trunk we had taken it for a pit-head lum. Above, far above, it blossomed into a billowing head of foliage. Once, it had paged the long-demobilised Kilmoggie Castle.

'What's up there?' asked the Doctor, like us prickling with horrid suspicion.

'Ma caat,' wailed Annie, 'ma caat....' and the appalling certainty dropped on us with eighteen claws. And dug in.

'Get it doon fer her,' demanded the first wifie, 'ye're climbers.' Voices from behind – 'Aye, ye're climbers, get it doon fer her.' An objectionable voice: 'Aye, and be some bluidy use fer once.'

But it was a terrifying tree. The Apprentice mumbled about the Fire Brigade. 'Fire Brigade? We canna get the Fire Brigade. It's twal mile th'ither side o Balweemie pittan oot fires.' 'Aye, fires stertit by campers,' spat out another wifie, evidently in the B & B business. They were not really hostile, just rightfully resentful of our intense desire to be elsewhere. Fortunately, we did not suggest the Polis. But we continued to dither. To strengthen a sense of commitment, the boy and some companions dumped our gear, looted from the bar, below the trunk. 'There y'are.'

Murmurs of approval. Multiple despatch of spittle.

Annie grabbed the Doctor's unsteady arm. 'Mebbe ye're no used tae climban trees, eh?' He looked gratefully at her. 'There's ladders....' –

she turned round – 'Pit thae ladders thegither,' she yelled. A formidable crone, and crafty.

The bole soared bald for forty feet. What ladders could reach that far? And an ash, the Doctor explained, was a very *unsympathetic* tree; the devil to climb. Horrible. Meanwhile, we searched the canopy. Helpful fingers pointed out various invisibilities. The Apprentice maintained that a beast bold enough and brainless enough to climb up there was equally well equipped to climb down again. 'Ah, but cats, cats,' sighed the Doctor, '...particularly young ones. Is this a young cat? 'he asked Annie, playing for time.

'Na, na, an auld yin: Tammas.' Tammas had done this before, when the Fire Brigade was not otherwise occupied, and his retrieval had become a local classic. Two firemen, it seemed, finished up in hospital. The outcome of his second expedition was therefore awaited with interest.

While the several ladders were being lashed, hammered and cursed together, the Rescue Team was disputing Honours. The Doctor emphasised that advanced modern techniques were required, and therefore the Apprentice was the logical choice; he himself would be worse than useless. The Apprentice, while conceding the latter point for most situations, compared a tree with the vegetated routes so beloved of the Doctor; our affair on The Craggie still rankled. He explained it was ideal for the Doctor – '... Vegetation all round, like a sea-stack of leaves, an Old Man of Chlorophyll – perfect.' 'No, it's purely...'

'Wheesht!' roared a large elderly man beside us. Sibilances rippled away. Hush.

We heard the wind beating the upper branches. Then a yowl; a small windblown yowl, but undeniably from a cat. Up there. Damnation.

'Here y'are, Jimmy!' cried our companion, slapping the Doctor's long-suffering shoulder. A gang of youths, who would have been better employed climbing the thing, were pushing a wavering company of ladders up the trunk of the tree. Four ancient wooden eight-footers, tied in line with minimal overlap. They collapsed drunkenly, and began to slide sideways. They were hauled back by knotted washing-line. A large splinter fell heavily, not from the tree.

'Jump on them, lads, it'll haud them doon!'

Some of the gathering mistook our hesitation. 'Ah, ye'd like fine tae climb it straucht aff, eh? Mair the thing, like? Na, na, tak the ladder's far as ye can. There's plenty climban fer yese efter that!' True.

The Apprentice trod the scaffold first. With a succession of slings, he bound the lower ladders to the trunk. They protested wheezily. When he ran short of slings an old body took a knife to our two 50-metre coils. This drove us all up the rungs, clutching equipment. We spiralled the ladders with precious kernmantel.

It was terrifying. Quite vertical. Rounded exiguous rungs, some missing, others rotten, slobbered against wet bark (rain had arrived to watch, as well). The trunk was much too broad to clasp, the ladder sides were loose and slippery. Looking down, the eye bounced off the bole and plunged into a flutter of white faces.... Surely the whole thing was toppling....

Above, the Apprentice, unconquerable, had left the topmost rung and was jerking one sling up the greasy pole inch by inch while leaning out from another. Then he clipped into the upper sling and repeated the process, coaxing the lower one above the upper. He pressed against pitons, deep into secondary thickening. Some fifteen feet were ascended this way, and darkness was closing in. Then, after two shots, he lassoed the lowest bough, fixed a line, and jumared aloft. Murmurs. Approbation at last. The Doctor called up to reserve the first coconut.

I reached the top of the ladder, sea-sick. Then a cry from the Apprentice – 'There's the brute!' And the rope whisked away. I hung out to watch. He was advancing, on hands and knees, along a large horizontal bough, preceded by the cat walking backwards. Each time he stopped to fix a runner on the branch above, the cat stopped. When he resumed, the cat resumed. The bough got thinner, and bent downwards. Both contestants began to wobble, but continued grimly towards the end. Clearly the Rescue would not come off; the Apprentice or the cat, or both, almost certainly would. If the cat – and, judging from the hate on the Apprentice's visage, that seemed likely – then lynching would ensue; enough rope, plenty of branches. So I, at centre of communication, managed to convey the logical (and convenient) solution that now the ropework was fixed, the Doctor, with his kind cat-loving heart, should replace the venomous Apprentice.

The cat, perched on a bouncing spray of twiggery, surveyed the resulting gymnastics without comment. Darkness had fallen, and we

were smokily floodlit from below by an old roaring break-down van. Drama was intense, as the Doctor, slithering desperately despite clinkers, edged towards Tammas. Employing all his vegetatious skills, he wriggled from fingertips to bootlaces.

We could not hear his blandishments, but they probably resembled those squandered on the climbing dog of Arran (a day of pleasure compared to this).

The branch dipped further. The Doctor began to slip. He shuffled backwards. His face was pale and petrified in the lamp beam; shining black branches scampered about him, sluicing water. Rain pelted.

It could not continue. It did not. The bough suddenly cracked and bent double, the Doctor, head down, heels up, swung under and wrapped himself about it like a newly-licensed sloth. The wee beastie, now below him, summoned its remaining lives and skedaddled upwards. It prepared to crampon daintily across his white streaming face. It paused, sprang at the bergschrund – and the Doctor grabbed.

He caught the cat, but lost the bough. He hung upside down by his knees for a long millisecond: and then gracefully slid off into the air.

Perlon plinged, we heard a snap above wind and engine, and a couple of runners broke free; twigs and leaves fluttered through the beam. But he stopped, spinning well below the bough and thirty feet above the ground. He was still clutching a small black object which even at that distance radiated fury.

We expected applause; or, at the least, pity and terror. But no. A degree of censure.

'Auld fule fell aff!' (the Doctor, not Tammas). 'Sayan they wis climbers....' 'Micht hae killt the beast....' 'Should hae left it tae the young lad....' 'I telt ye, they're no...' Annie, however, was peering up with a diabolical grin. 'Hey, Tammas, Tammas!' she cried. Tammas was no doubt longing for the relative security of a broomstick.

We faced logistics. The Apprentice explored, wreathed in ropes. He appeared and vanished among ebony branchwork, trailing ghostly loops through snatches of floodlight. Beneath him, the Doctor twirled, with his outraged burden. Tammas had lost dignity; and hell hath no fury like a cat so bereft. He held the creature now close, now at arm's length. Either way, he was being rapidly abraded. He could not be pulled up; and he could not abseil while acting as male nurse.

The Apprentice therefore threw down a length of light line for the little one. The Doctor was to tie him on it and lower him to Annie's bony grasp. This proved difficult, Tammas being a bonnie fechter and wet and slippery. 'Round its bloody neck!' roared the Apprentice, thoroughly fed up. But humanity prevailed, and a sort of Tammas splint was conjured by the Doctor and his foe secured, tail wrapped tight like a muffler.

Then the bulb blew in the floodlight. Pandemonium. When light returned it revealed a smaller rotating object below the larger one. Tammas, no hand – or paw – at abseils, had stuck. His line was jammed under the sodden capstan of coils above the Doctor. The Apprentice could not help, for his own branch was splitting. He retreated and tied the Doctor to a higher limb. But that didn't get Tammas down, and until that object had achieved its owner's skinny bosom we dared not descend ourselves.

The Doctor, from his gyrations, shouted for the crane of the break-down truck; Tammas, counter-gyrating below, joined in through tail. At top elevation, the crane might just... Smoke and fumes, roars; a bold figure swarmed up its hiccupping vertebrae and held out hands. About five feet short.... The Doctor *could* cut the line; but if Tammas missed, he would be sure, that night, to break his neck.

The figure smote its brow, scrambled down and vanished into the crowd, which was boiling up to an Ibrox. He reappeared carrying a great salmon net, doubtless veteran of many another night. On tiptoe at full stretch of crane he could just tickle the enraged Tammas' toes.

'Right!' And the Doctor leaned over and sawed at the line. A fearful hush. The motor paused and the beam flickered.

Then, plop! He was landed. Right in the net. Deafening cheers, hoots, screams, whistles.... Goal. Everybody stormed the pitch.

Well, we got the Doctor down, too, eventually. But no one stayed to watch. They bore Annie and the tightly-knitted Tammas off into darkness. Fortunately, they left our light on.

We shouldered gear and trudged up the lane. We were sore, soaked, and the bar would be shut. A door opened and a blaze leapt out, the truck driver after it. The Doctor thanked him for his light. To our surprise, he enveloped us all in an ample grasp.

'Come awa in, boys, come awa in, we're aa waitan on yese....'

And they were. A memorable night, till late early morning. Unlimited food, drink, music and song. The salmon-netter buttoned an accordion wonderfully, the Amazonian wifie – a Higgins in more itinerant days – gave splendidly belligerent renderings of *The Blantyre Explosion* and *The Donibristle Disaster*; the Apprentice of course indulged to wild applause in *Great John MacLean*, Annie herself piercingly to even wilder in *Andra Lammie*; the Doctor tried out his new reel 'Black Diamonds' on a borrowed chanter bent like a pit-prop – there were marvellous stories and some scarifying wit – but I remember little. I do remember how they plastered the Doctor's slashes, scratches, bites and bruises with an emotional rhetoric of iodine. 'Terrible, terrible.' 'It's thae *claws*; an thae *teeth*.' 'An he *needna* hae done it.' 'He did it fer Annie.' 'No fer the bluidy cat, onywye'...

Tammas, rebuilding dignity, had sought his dubious blanket. We asked how he had so badly mauled the firemen that they had to go to hospital. 'It wisna Tammas.' Had they fallen off their ladders, then? 'Na, na.' 'What?' 'They wis jist fou.' They had fallen out of their fire engine's door, waving unbelted as it roared away after the previous Kilmoggie Gathering. 'Three weeks in hospital, man. Aa fer auld Annie's Tammas.... But they get *paid* for it, ken; they're no like Climbers....'

See what I mean?

We slept on the salmon-netter's bed till six o'clock.

MIDGES

Midges have been much maligned. They not only protect us, provide an unsleeping Air Umbrella for our precious West Highland scenery: they can also help us to a First Ascent – or to understand what a First Ascent is really about. They are great teachers of ethics. As we discovered to our cost. Although we made that First Ascent – the Best-Seller of its day – with the help of midges, we were ashamed of ourselves, the Apprentice and I; we still are.

Yet, as a Munro is a Munro, so a First Ascent is a First Ascent, and nowadays nobody is perfect; moreover, the germ, so to speak, of this biological weapon emanated from the Doctor, hitherto so upright a man. He was not in the climbing team – the grade was too high – he was Base for the expedition; Base indeed. But he ensured our success; if it can be called a success when the vanquished, however disreputable, trudge off with the moral victory.

Enough of snivelling. To the story. It is a lesson for all climbers. It should be told. For, as the Doctor observed by the primus that evening, peering into his glass through a penumbra of equally thirsty uncountables: 'Too much competition – *poogh* – tends to obscure the – *poogh* – essential Spirit.'

The Apprentice had to cross to Harris for that first ascent. His fellow-Weasels were Alpineering and rivals were athirst. So I joined him; the crux coming last, I could at worst be hauled over it. The Doctor was there to cook, and watch the fun.

The weather steamed close and cloudy, after weeks of cold rain. We waded over a sopping hill, and the great cliff Sròn a' Mheanbh-Chuileag rose imperturbably before us. Our eyes scurried nervously about it. No one was there. We would be first! Straight up the centre unrolled the only possible line, Leac Mhòr, the Great Slab, that unclimbed new discovery everyone was raving about. It had been attempted only the week before by a couple of teams but, as the Apprentice pointed out, they came from Glasgow. They had, nevertheless, pioneered as far as the crux. *That* appeared impossible – it jerked outwards above us like a vast flight of stone steps seen upside down from underneath.

'Great,' declared the Apprentice, a little hoarsely.

We splashed down to the river gravel for a meal. Our domestic help began to make jammy pieces and set up the tent. The Apprentice and I, adhesive from sweat and apprehension, stripped and plunged into a fine bellowing pool, frothy with spate.

'Don't!' called the Doctor. 'It's dangerous!'

We looked at each other. We had all of us forded and swum (often by accident) much fiercer water than this. The Doctor had now turned not only cook but nursemaid. Nonsense. Perfectly safe.

'The midges!' he shouted. 'They'll get you when you come out.'

So what? We two were going up the Slab, not festering round the tent like him.

As we munched our pieces, vastly refreshed, and insulated by the Doctor's unseen rucksack from infinite bog, we ridiculed his prognosis. Ah, but immersion, he averred, removed the body's protective layer of oils. 'You mean dirt?' suggested the Apprentice, through his crumbs. 'Exactly!' It appeared that the accumulated greases of the skin impeded midgy mandibles. They found it difficult to sook. Washed, we would be a naked lunch to innumerable multitudes of *Ceratopogonidae*. This place in this weather would generate the most ravenous midges within the whole lengthy jurisdiction of An Comhairle nan Eilean. The Doctor had already identified them as the two worst of the whole bloodsucking bunch, *Culicoides heliophilus* and *Culicoides impunctatus*. So there.

A few of the brutes had already appeared that morning. They bit us even in our then well-enough-larded state. As the old man at the last croft had remarked, 'The midges is no very good the day.' So we rubbed in more midge-repellent and hurried across to the climb, the Doctor remaining entrenched behind turned-up collar, pipe smoke and Natural Oils.

I do not want to remember the rest of that day. Instead of climbing out of midges, we climbed into them. The Sròn was the west end of a high boggy tableland, its top and sides dribbled with bog; it stood in a bog. So, from bottom, sides and top midges screamed out at us, radars blaring, rockets firing. Faces, hair, necks, ears, eyes, backs of hands, wrists, crawled with a million engines, tracers incessantly stung and flashed. Torture of infinite needles. Jab, jab, jab. Hell, hell, hell; more hell....

I gave up half-way, blind and one-handed. The Apprentice lasted a little longer, banging in a runner at the crux. But he ran out of oaths, and midges swarmed into the vacated territory. We spun down, coiled ropes and vanished. Flies were nothing to this.

At the tent, we dived into bags, head and all. The Doctor, puffing valiantly, made supper. Midge-netting kept most outside, and those within – chastened by St. Bruno – congregated along the ridge-seams and were periodically incinerated by a brandished Primus. Numbers gradually decreased. We uncovered heads, warily.

'Midges no very good the day,' observed our companion genially, poking the pot. He remained unchastised, for cooks are the Sacred Fools of climbing, licensed jesters, dear to the belly. And he had warned us.

That night, sleep was fitful; we were iridescent with bites, and refugees wandered wakefully about our hair. The Apprentice tossed, in a rage of frustration. First ascent ... first ascent ... and last chance.

We rose late, to a midgeless morning. But the steamy weather promised another yesterday. However, the Doctor had not been idle. He produced two midge-helmets for us: his spare stockings, with slits for eyes. 'And you can wear your own spare socks as gloves, the ends pierced for fingers.' That, and the remaining midge cream, would see us up to – maybe over – the crux, now the way there was familiar. We blessed him as he stirred the porridge, twinkling grand-maternally.

The Apprentice crawled out, stood up, and gazed happily at the Sròn. Then his eyes popped. He groaned, swore, stamped, slapped thighs and cursed again. We all peered out.

Below the crag stood People. We were forestalled. Who?

'No, no; Oh NO!' wailed the Apprentice. 'It's *them*!'

'Who's Them?' asked the Doctor, beginning to regret his slit stockings.

'Wee Dander', sobbed the Apprentice, '*and* Greetin Jimmie; *and* The Porpus.' He named three legendary figures. 'And there's Else and Big Ian to look after them....'

We were suitably silent. Wee Dander was one of those youthful prodigies who – for a few years – climb apparently everything with unstopping ease and no little scorn. More than that, he would never write up his routes, never bother to record them. He had no use for journals or guidebooks, or other people. He was pure Oral Tradition, pure Hero, sheer Me; free as the wind. Hateful, no doubt; but enviable in many ways. His companions tied themselves always second and third on a rope that was invariably the best you could buy, like the rest of his kit – which he never did buy: the three of them, aided by Else and Big Ian, took whatever they needed from any unoccupied tent or car they came across. Hateful. Dangerously enviable.

They saw us and ambled over as we swallowed our now tasteless porridge. Wee Dander was indeed wee, a laddie, in tatty shirt and shorts, with an open expressionless very pale face and uncannily penetrating blue eyes; any age between twelve and seventeen. He bent over and picked a piece of bacon from the pan the Doctor was frying and nibbled it carefully. Then he picked a couple more pieces and threw them to his companions behind. All three masticated in silence.

We looked them over, refusing to speak first. Greetin Jimmie was a long skeletal youth in grubby denims and greasy shirt; his equally oleaginous hair sprawled to a thin pimply face, dreepy red nose and sparse fringe of unappetizing gingery beard – or he may not have shaved that week (it was indeed difficult to imagine him shaving). A dismal enough streak, from knocky knees to watery eyes. The Porpus – round and polished as the playful Cetacean – bulged from relatively clean sark and shorts; he grinned even while chewing, small pink nose and ears oscillating independently. He rolled an enormous boulder across and sat on it; it was one the Doctor and I had failed to shift when pitching the tent.

Before Wee Dander could appropriate more breakfast the Doctor smartly tossed the rest to us. Our guest was then moved to communicate.

'Saw yer runner. Been up, eh?' A hard, clear, raw-fish accent.

The Apprentice, wrestling with honesty, said he'd had a look and come down early, but would be up the day right enough.

'Like hell.' (Pause) 'But thanks fer the runner; nae use here – 'll dae fine fer the Ben next week, though.' (Pause) 'Well, we'll jist awa up. See ya.'

And he sauntered off back to the cliff. Greetin Jimmie nodded morosely at us and followed his leader. The Porpus, still managing the odd chew, beamed and waved a flipper. He clanked away uphill; they were particularly well-equipped that morning, having passed a Mountain Adventure camp the day before.

They paused at our pool. The Porpus gesticulated. He wished to gambol therein. Wee Dander scowled: and was moving away when the Doctor, to our astonishment, leapt up and shouted.

'Hi! Don't go in! It's dangerous....'

What the devil? We looked at him bewildered; then at the three. But the Doctor knew his man. Wee Dander stopped dead. His eyes unslung their Kalashnikovs. He was not going to be head-mastered by any what-ho! tweed-brandishing establishmentarian.

He stripped off and dived, right into the considerable whirlie under the waterfall; and stayed down a long while to prove his point. The Porpus rolled and splashed, gleaming epidermally, while Jimmie, even dirtier with his clothes off, waded in slowly, rubbing long thin shanks bitterly and fading gradually to a pale shrimp-pink.

The Apprentice smiled for the first time in twenty-four hours. That, of course, is why we climb with the Doctor. A practical man, so *good* with People.

We took it easy. We watched them rope up; we saw Big Ian and Else unfold some sort of encampment on the bog beneath the cliff. We kitted ourselves out, packing midge-helmets and socks carefully, and used up all the midge cream so we needn't tell a lie later. The Doctor stayed to guard the tent. We strolled across in the gathering fug, regarding emergent midges almost benignly. Of course we were a little dirtier now, more naturally repellent....

Wee Dander proved a marvellous climber. He was already entering the crux. He would easily get over, he contemptuously pocketed the Apprentice's sling, he flowed with a lovely movement, elastic as rubber. Greetin Jimmie stalked after him like a vertical pond-skater; multilimbed, impeccably adept. The Porpus, whose job was never to peel but to hold the others when they did, scuttled like a crab. It was a great team to watch. We felt ourselves almost wishing them success.

Then they began to jerk, increasingly. Early Warnings had sounded, the defenders were busy. Progress slowed, became intermittent. The rope twitched agonizingly; coiled, uncoiled, gave forth sobs and cries. It was not so nice to watch. A beautiful animal was being done to death. The leader crouched between moves, slapped bare thighs and neck, his second agitated beneath a cloud, the third man beat bongo-drums about his waist-band, jangling in disarray.

We came up to Else, a plump vaguely belligerent Amazon, and Big Ian, even larger and grinning hugely. 'Bloody midges,' he remarked, rubbing with vigour. What went on above was not of great concern to him. Else swore low and continuously, rummaging in an ample knee-length jersey, well adapted to supermarkets.

A great crash above us, and we all fled. Wee Dander, blinded by midgery, had peeled on the final step. Greetin Jimmie, enmeshed in his web, shot up – still scratching – to a sentry box. The Porpus, smacking his backside, sat down in space and held them all; a large sling of Mountain Adventure cutlery had meanwhile slipped off his tray and nearly brained us.

It was a curious sight; three in tension at various angles, writhing and scratching like St. Vitus. Somehow, Wee Dander fought back up, Jimmie slithered down to his stance, The Porpus swam to the surface. But all magic was gone. The lower pair, fisting eyes, faces and limbs in a frenzy, implored their leader to come down. Wee Dander tried again. And again; wiping his forehead – milling with millions – blindly against the cold Precambrian. Terrifying. At the very profile of the last step we watched him slip, slip, recover; slip, recover.

Then he abseiled down. And, yes; we were sorry.

They stood beside us, two of them rubbing and cursing. Wee Dander, his pale face bloodstained, crawling with tormentors, looked straight at us. His teeth had bitten his lips white.

'Any ... midge ... cream ... ?' It must have cost him.

We had used all ours up, the Apprentice explained. He displayed the flattened tube. He did not look at me; nor I at him. Silence.

'Aye,' said Wee Dander.

Else and Big Ian had packed up the tents. They all moved off, hunched and muffled, pummelling zipped anoraks, Wee Dander leading. He slowed, the others overtook him. He stopped, looked back and spun something towards us.

'Yer runner,' he said. And went on.

We deserved it.

MIDSUMMER MADNESS

'Scotland is nowadays quite impossible! No peace any more: Always somebody messing about somewhere....'

This Doctorial outburst summed up our feelings. It was midsummer night – or eve, an all-night eve – on a Monadhliath top, a bump in the plateau. Miles, we had hoped, from anywhere; or anybody. We had camped there, after climbing on Creag Mhòr at Kingussie, just for the pleasure of doing nothing but laze, seeing nothing but the low rim of the northern sun beyond Wyvis – and perhaps a passing herd of deer; and hearing nothing but the occasional sough of wind to round off the silence – and maybe the cry of a distant bird. Aaaah.... Wonderful....

Instead, we had been disturbed by distressingly human shouts and shrieks, mingled with bugle calls and horn-blowings, that emanated apparently from every innocently humped summit about us. Swearing, we had peered beyond the tent flaps and witnessed lights flashing signals; and made out an occasional bowed and plodding figure against the rolling black horizon. Military exercises? Boys' Brigade? Nocturnal Munroists?

We had just pulled up our bags again after one such infuriating alarm, when the tent guys sang suddenly, and a guttural cry made us sit up. Immediately afterwards, the walls billowed inward and the Doctor was flung hard against the pole. We scrambled out, torches blazing in wrath.

Yes, some idiot had walked into the tent. With the whole deserted tableland to wander about in, he had to – walk into our tent. We fixed him severely with indignant beams.

He was a small man in a thin grey suit; around him lay long poles, balls of string, parcels and rolls of paper. And – a bugle. He looked unhappy. Shocked, in fact. To be fair, he in his turn no doubt did not expect, stumbling by dark across the summit plateau of the Monadhliaths, to have walked into a tent. But what the devil was he doing there himself, transporting such an odd assemblage of property in the middle of the night? Surely not... flitting?

We dragged him into the tent, revived him with Doctorial whisky and, since sleep was now impossible, brewed some tea.

When he seemed more in the world, we interrogated him. What on earth was he doing here?

'I'm looking for my wife.'

'Your wife?'

'Yes. Mrs Urania Grey-Mullett; you know....'

We did not know. Was she lost?

'Oh no, not at all.' We fancied a note of regret. 'She's been on Càrn Sgùlain, she's to meet me here at Càrn Ballach, and my daughter as well – she's coming from Càrn Dearg. And Edward, from A' Chailleach.'

Heavens, this was a Waterloo Place, a Charing Cross. 'I suppose you're all collecting Munros', observed the Doctor testily, striving for politeness.

But George – that was his name – George Grey-Mullett did not appear familiar with Munros.

'We've just been taking sightings,' he explained. 'Mrs Grey-Mullett, as I expect you are aware, is extending her studies to this part of the Highlands.' We were not aware; incomprehension remained mutual. We swallowed our tea and surveyed his pile of maps and poles. He began to tell us about his wife, about his daughter, about Edward, and about the studies that threatened to extend across our once solitary encampment.

His explanations were interrupted every five minutes – by his watch – with rushing outside to the summit cairn and flashing a large torch, followed by a melancholy toot on his bugle; then waiting for answering flashes and wails from his companions as they toiled up their respective slopes towards us. In between, we gathered that Mrs Grey-Mullett was an authority – or had made a name for herself – on prehistoric astro-nomical-observatory sites among the hills. Something after the fashion of Professor Thom, of whom the Doctor had once been so tiresome a fan. By sighting the sun, or moon, or stars, along cairns or pointed boulders or summit nicks, our forefathers could deduce the date: how near they were to important agriculturo-religious (George pronounced this twice for our benefit, with a sip between) agriculturo-religious festivals that punctuated the year and stabilised their society. Mrs Grey-Mullett had a knack, not only of lining up her sightings, but of identifying – in just the right places – the stones and slabs indubitably employed for kneeling on to take your observation, or for sacrificing your Sacred Victim. It required great skill – he might say intuition, also – to distinguish these man-made artifacts, smoothed by thousands of years of weathering, from casual effects of wind, water or Ice Age. And considerable knowledge. Mrs Grey-Mullett, if not perhaps a practising devotee of, was nevertheless very well instructed about, the Triple Goddess.

'All that bloody rot....' commented the Apprentice rudely, wiping his mouth of tea. We had suffered enough Professor Thom, Golden Boy Frazer, and of course Robert Graves. 'Loonie stuff.' But, as the Doctor more kindly observed, stirring up the porridge (for it was now clearly dawn), Midsummer Eve seemed an appropriate date to encounter the White Goddess: her real house-parties took place at this time.

George nodded, his face serious. '*And* at mid-winter.... Ah, I hear my wife now,' he added, and rose stiffly. We crawled outside.

We all heard Mrs Grey-Mullett. The earth shook.

The sun, already high in the east, was temporarily eclipsed as the lady climbed on to the summit above us. Mr Grey-Mullett raised his bugle and blew. A brazen blast replied, and his wife descended upon us, flumping in a thick tweed skirt, anorak and purple woolly bonnet. She stopped, slung her trumpet behind her, and peered closely.

'Why, Doctor!' she boomed, 'Doctor!' 'Urania Major!' gasped our companion, 'Lord, I haven't seen you, it must be, these twenty years, never dreamed...' Much mutual hand-clasping and arm-slapping. She turned out to be a sister of Ursula, the Mrs Cairnwhapple, M.B.O.U., whom we had met, booming as imperially, on Lochnagar during the Pitfoulie episode. Equally bulky, Urania too began as a birdwatcher – had indeed cornered her husband in a cramped nocturnal hide at Loch Skinaskink; but now followed more substantial quarry – stones and slabs, cairns and megaliths; and George had become her chief assistant – or porter, it seemed. He carried things. 'George used to be in Rateable Values', she explained, 'but I made him retire early; he is so Useful.'

One of his uses had been to sire her daughter, who now appeared from her own particular cairn; a fine bouncy blonde, a Spring version of her Midsummer mother. 'Hi-yi!' she carolled: 'God: who are all these people?' Her mother explained, and introduced us: to... Blod... Blodeuwedd. An old Welsh name for the Goddess as Maiden, Mrs

Grey-Mullett assured us. 'Most attractive, isn't it? George wished to call her Mary, after some aunt of his, but we just keep that as a second name.' We boggled at the spelling, but the Doctor, who as a boy had scrambled extensively with his uncle among the hills, valleys, double consonants and two-faced vowels of North Wales, performed the task expertly. ('Wonderful language – spelling perfectly phonetic'). We could not even pronounce it. 'You can call me Bloody, if you like – or Bloody Mary,' conceded her daughter, 'most people do.' '*Bloddy*, dear,' protested George, feeling among his parcels for sandwiches.

So we ate our strange breakfast together. There was no sign of Edward. 'Edward', announced Mrs Grey-Mullett disapprovingly, 'has had to go home. I expect he's Found Something.' She munched bacon rolls. 'He's always doing that.' Edward was an Archaeologist. 'Mother discovered him in an Earth-house in Fife', explained Blodeuwedd, 'and raised him to higher things.' His hobby, indeed, was Hawking.

'A dreadful nuisance, when he brings his – what d'you call it, Bloddy? – anyway, his wretched bird on the hill with us. He also', she added as an afterthought, 'speaks Pictish.' We gaped, as much at a loss for words as any dictionary of that much postulated tongue.

Over our meal we were treated to an exposition concerning the religious festivities associated with the midsummer solstice, once its date had been fixed along the lines drawn out by Mrs Grey-Mullett. The victims – Sacred Kings of the Waxing Year – were of course always male. They had been for six months consorts of the Goddess, in the glamorous person of her young Chief Priestess, before being flayed, impaled, thrown over a cliff, burnt, drowned, buried alive, eaten or otherwise ritually and entertainingly disposed of by their successors.

'But always', explained Mrs Grey-Mullett, 'castrated first. A bronze sickle. For fertility, for the crops. Afterwards, naturally, they became immortal.' She chewed bacon roll dreamily. 'Wonderful times to have lived in,' she sighed. Blodeuwedd nodded, munching, and unwrapped a Mars Bar with care. The Doctor scraped his pan. 'Human nature,' he noted, 'remains much the same.' The Apprentice and I thought of discussing Rateable Values with George; but he was asleep among his parcels.

The lady continued to address us and the nearer Monadhliaths. Winter, it seemed, the Grey-Mulletts devoted to theory; drawing lines and conclusions. 'But in summer, it's Practicalities, isn't it, Blodeuwedd? Stern practicalities.'

They finished their meal. Mrs Grey-Mullett briskly rubbed her hands on a napkin; George obediently tidied away.

'Now, we should not disturb you, Doctor, but we must look at our maps and rule in a few more sightings: there is a wind getting up – do you mind if we spread things out in your tent for a little while?' We escaped, before engulfment in George's unfolding preparations.

Within, the lady boomed; her husband tapped his calculator. We looked at each other. Then at Bloddy, who was seated, decoratively, on a rucksack and still eating chocolate. She stretched shapely shorts; and a shapely smile. The Apprentice, reassured, proffered his spare bar. She took it, and patted the rucksack beside her invitingly. Our companion, mesmerised, moved across. He would last, doubtless, until the 22nd of December, if George got his sums right.

They seemed right. Mrs Grey-Mullett emerged, beaming. She had again been proved correct. Càrn Ballach was a *most* important observational site. 'The name itself suggests that.' But surely Ballach is named after bealach, a pass? 'No, no, all these are *modern* corruptions – the last fifteen hundred years or so. Ballach is really from Beli (Baal, you know) which is from Belili, the Goddess' name in her very powerful Pig Form. We nearly called Blodeuwedd after Belili, the Sow Goddess; but it could have been unfortunate at school. Now, this area has possibly the greatest number of *Càrn* names in Scotland, look at them here.' She rattled out the map and reeled them off. '*Sixteen* contained within these *three* alignments (*three* for the Triple Goddess), sixteen being the number of Increase, besides being made up of *nine* (three threes) and the sacred number *seven* (days, planets, candlesticks)...' George interrupted with a correction: 'Ah, *fifteen*, my dear, that extra cairn is fly-dirt, the true summit is just outside the alignment.' The lady changed into third gear and continued unabashed, 'Well, *fifteen*. *Fifteen* is of course the number of letters in the Ogham alphabet they would have used, made up of *three* times *five*, the five fingers, Dactyls, the Five-Fold Knot for tying the Victim....'

Mrs Grey-Mullett would have been great, running a Bingo Hall or presenting Treasury Estimates. We thought of the fruitful opportunities she had (so far) ignored: the numbers of the Ordnance map sheets, their editions, the Grid References, positions in the Munros list, altitudes in feet and metres. But she plunged on.

'*Càrn* is of course from a Mediterranean form of the Goddess, Carnea – another name for Artemis, the child-eater. You see, the Sacred Kings later on postponed their Immortality a little while by employing child surrogates.' The Doctor ventured, but was brushed aside. 'No, *Càrn* is not from heaps of stones: the heaps of stones are named from Carnea. Now then, look at these *three* cairns on the map here (three again, you see), all in a straight line, pointing – when you have corrected for star movements and changes in the earth's rotational axis over the past few thousand years – due north, to Corona Borealis, where the Sacred King goes after death: Càrn Ballach, Càrn Mor, Càrn Leachtar Dhubh – and lining up *exactly* with that charming sacrificial stone we found in Gaick, remember, Bloddy?'

Eventually we retrieved our tent and packed up, Mr Grey-Mullett popping in and out to collect rubbers and tracing paper. The Apprentice trod on a ruler and snapped it. 'No matter', said Mr Grey-Mullett, philosophically.

No matter, indeed. You could draw straight lines through any three of the multitudes of local *Càrns* in a heavily-stalked area like this; every pony-boy had built one. But we held our peace.

The Grey-Mulletts huddled in discussion. They summoned us. The lady explained that Edward's desertion now threatened to spoil an exciting follow-up: another sighter was needed. Just for the day. 'Someone to run about and do little things with Blodeuwedd: George and I are getting too old and stiff these days.'

The Apprentice needed no encouragement. He would love to do little things with Blodeuwedd. The Doctor and I watched them troop off to the next top. We heard Bloddy's fruity laughter. We wondered if our reckless companion would ever return. Fortunately, he had never given us the impression of being particularly Sacred.

The day continued fine, and late that afternoon we admired the view, coming down into Gleann Ballach. A mile further on, a bounding figure hailed us: Blodeuwedd, hair streaming behind her like molten gold in the long lazy light.

'Mother says will you come and see something Very Interesting? Just up on the right.'

We went. A few hundred yards, and Mrs Grey-Mullett reared herself, stag-like, majestically from the heather.

'Ah, Doctor, now I can show you something! Just where I calculated it would be! Here on one side we have Càrn Dearg – the red cairn, red for death and blood, you see; and there on the other, A' Chailleach – the Old Woman, the Goddess as Hag, reinforced by Geal Chàrn – the Goddess as White Carnea! And right between them on the subsidiary line – a splendid example of my Class IIA displacement – where the rising sun shines down from the north-east: what do we find but this – a perfectly lovely little Sacrificial Slab! Now look at it carefully – this is where the priestesses knelt, a depression each side – see – for their knees, so they could hold the victim – drugged of course. There is the incised Spiral of Immortality. And here the little scoop to collect the blood. And this flat stone I've just cleared, is where the chief priestess would stand holding the dagger – or the sickle – in her hand. Quite, quite delightful!'

The Apprentice lay stretched on the slab, wearing a ghastly grin. Mr Grey-Mullett, as priestess, calmed him. Blodeuwedd took up her position, holding the most crooked of the Apprentice's pitons, anticipatory as Steffi Graf before the net. Mrs Grey-Mullett circled them hypnotically with a camera, no doubt subconsciously repeating the movements of the Crane Dance – *nine* steps and a leap. She reassured the Victim. 'No, lie quite relaxed. Don't try to smile, there's a good boy, I want it to look *realistic*.' She clicked from various angles. The Doctor and I cackled, safe on the periphery.

Then the ceremony was over. The red-faced Apprentice resurrected himself, dusting his breeks. He had not, it seemed, acted as surrogate for the Sacred King; this was only a minor slab, for an everyday kind of victim. No great calendar event, just a checking of the tribal clock. Mr Grey-Mullett scribbled notes, possibly on the low Rateable Value of this particular site of immolation.

The ladies had a few more little things to do; the Apprentice meekly departed with them. George was returning to prepare the evening meal in their campavan. We went down with him, being parked at the same road-end.

Two hours later, the midsummer twilight had still not illuminated any of the three. Mr Grey-Mullett shook his head; she must really have got stuck into something. 'Her studies, you know, go very deep.' He would wait there, anyway; we should walk back up – just to see. He lent us his bugle affair. He offered tuition: 'Screw up your lips like this – then grunt: *Booo!*'

We had almost reached the site of the photogenic sacrifice, with no sign or sound. We climbed fallen boulders below the face of Càrn Dearg and gazed about; self-consciously, we wound our lonely horn. Only echoes.

Yet one echo seemed persistent. We trailed it, blowing – or grunting – determinedly. Yes, it grew to independent tootling, and appeared to issue from below ground.

We pushed aside bracken and bony heather, among the piled rocky debris, injecting our two and a half notes into dark cavernous cracks and fissures.

At last we stood over a peculiarly jumbled crevasse system, an eviscerated stone whale. Mournful hoots percolated from beneath. Then voices, gusts of laughter. The Apprentice and Bloddy were within. They had discovered – at the end of another of Mrs Grey-Mullett's alignments – what seemed to be a tunnel to a burial chamber, and followed it. They found the chamber. They were in it. But now they could not get out. Why?

'Because Mother's in the way!' The Doctor and I stared at each other. 'Yes, she came in after us, and' – shrieks of undaughterly mirth; the Apprentice took over. 'The old b-, the old lady – ', slappings, more giggling – 'got stuck. Her backside jammed with the trumpet under the lintel....'

We busied about and found the entrance. We had to make it an exit. The delicate task of sounding out the hindquarters and trumpet of Mrs Grey-Mullett, and of suitably easing them both backwards as undamaged as possible, was best left to my clinical colleague. I shone the operating torch. Various particles of clothing, and a trumpet, surgically removed from the hindquarters, were handed out; and I discreetly retired as the Doctor emerged backwards, followed by ample billows of pink and a chokeful of exclamations.

When I returned, they were all recovering from their collective inhumation, like something by Stanley Spencer. A trumpet and a horn were deployed apocalyptically about. Mrs Grey-Mullett sat, still fanning herself and puffing with emotion, draped informally below with strips of skirt and anorak. The Apprentice was blinking and mopping his brow, and La Belle Dame, completely without *merci*, loudly chaffed the Doctor as she beat earth out of her shorts and smoothed her dangerous hair. Clearly, he was to be the next victim.

Fortunately it was almost dark on the way down, and we gallantly walked in front of Mrs Grey-Mullet, who limped and jangled with safety-pins.

'We must come back and investigate that burial. I am convinced it is a burial.' It nearly had been, anyway.

'Doctor, do you think I'll be fit to crawl in there tomorrow, or should we leave it a little while? Do you advise that I should, in the meantime, try and reduce my, my *weight*? Bloddy, do stop fooling with that poor young man; I'm sure he's had enough of you, three hours in the same burial chamber.... Why, I myself could hardly breathe!'

All the way to Edinburgh, the Doctor and I chortled and the Apprentice sighed dreamily. Despite our cheap jokes, he kept silent. He was not going to enlighten the non-Elect about his Day-Return to the Underworld. He only remarked that if he had been sacrificed, he would at least have been Immortal, living with Blodeuwedd in the nine-gated Castle of the North Wind, eating an infinity of chocolate.

(Significantly, the journey from the burial chamber home took us *three* hours, *dead*. We had, however, stopped for chips at Dunkeld).

ACCESS

Ah, yes: access. That is a real problem.'

The Doctor shook his head and fingered his diminishing allowance of Highland Park. We were in Daddy McKay's, studying the map for next Saturday. The Doctor had been confined to his patients' beds for many a recent weekend, and we felt that this, his first free one, should be of his own choice.

To our politely-disguised chagrin, he had chosen Meall nam Fiaclan which, thanks to the regular orogenic free enterprise encouraged by the Ordnance Survey, had the previous year raised itself to Munro status.

As a result, it was being assailed every weekend by voracious hordes of metre-devourers, eager for more elevated fodder than weekday jogging could afford. As a further result, those unfortunate enough to farm, forest or shoot the lower slopes of Meall nam Fiaclan, a singularly isolated protuberance, had encompassed it with a Galvanised Iron Curtain. Approaches to the frontier bristled with barbs, swung with padlocks, blistered with exceedingly rude notices. Bulls, dogs and savagely uncomfortable retainers patrolled the fences.

Of course, one Route of Access had been discussed: that (the discussion) was only fair. The route was to be six feet wide, with no stepping off it. Ample; the Romans had run an Empire from only a few inches more. The trouble was that, naturally, none of the Owners would admit it might cross his particular land, and so its whereabouts – timidly signposted by various fund- and cap-raising Amenity Bodies – were bumped into, eased over or scornfully rubbed out by beast, bogey, bulldozer or busily underemployed whatnot. Wherever it went, it certainly would not take the only interesting way up Meall nam Fiaclan, a sort of craggy ridge that gave the heap its name; for that ridge rose above a very posh house indeed.

The Apprentice, numbly accepting the idea of walking up a Munro, warmed to the more attractive possibility of an Assault. The Doctor, to egg him on, read stirring accounts of climbing the Affric hills in the days of that dreadful American Mr Winans, when even the respectable had to skip delightedly from shelter to shelter beneath the telescopes swivelling daily from the ridge of Mam Soul.

We scanned the entry for Meall nam Fiaclan in the nervous little booklet on Access. Its message appeared clear enough. The Restricted Period ran, fairly comprehensively, from the 2nd April to the 31st March. The Owners' Names occupied half a page and read like an international Trotskyite hit-list – gone were those of our former doughty competitors, the double-barrelled English of both nationalities. The Preferred Route announced itself succinctly as 'None'; the Contact was a telephone number which no longer existed; the Remarks diplomatically concluded that 'an authorised footpath is under consideration.' It looked, as the Apprentice remarked, rather a good thing to tackle. We congratulated the Doctor. He beamed, called for the next round, and briefed us on the Order of Battle.

Following the dicta of Clausewitz, Liddell Hart, Guderian, Zhukhov and other internationally popular team managers, we were to attack where the defence least expected us. In this case, directly beneath that interesting ridge – straight up the fields beside the big posh house. Our General's temerity astonished us. The Apprentice, in his excitement, even paid for the Doctor's round.

'The point is', explained that military genius, 'Mowglie Castle has recently changed hands. The new chap's rather eccentric. Neighbours don't get on with him. Has queer ideas. Weak spot, eh? Name's pronounceable, too – Ulfsen; a Swede from Germany – a good honest European. Can't find much else about him except that he's a self-made man and doesn't like dogs: evicted all the old Sheikh's Rottweilers into the Canine Defence League. Should be no trouble of that sort, anyway.' As the Assault was to begin by night ('Much more fun; and they'll never expect us then'), we had worried about padding feet, hot breath and the odd fang. (We discussed further; but the rest of our debate is not yet Cleared for Publication).

We left the car a long way off, by the River Spray, with a wrapped-up tentpole like a fishing rod inside it to divert attention streamwards. When we climbed off the road to go over the top, we felt a tingling in the feet highly flattering to so humble a Munro of such recent creation. A mere V. Diff. took us through and over the barbs and mesh strung up by the old Sheikh to keep his doggywogs in. We were careful not to damage anything; sportsmanship is half the fun of battle; victory is sweeter to the chivalrous. These high-minded consolations of the criminal suffered severe abrasion during our next half hour among late-Arabian-now-Swedish Sitka spruce of southern Alaskan provenance; we decimated their infinite spears with xenophobic fury.

And emerged on to a wide, horribly open moonlit field. Above us rose Meall nam Fiaclan. On our left, pale gleaming turrets among tall timber. On our right, and beyond the field, a dark wood of similar trees.

The air smelt naked and ominous. Our necks prickled. And – surely that was a distant bark, or – even – howl, in the silence? We imagined paddings, breathings. We looked round; and round again. Nothing. 'Ulfsen hates dogs,' insisted the Doctor hoarsely; he obviously felt the same as we did. Our genes manned Action Stations.

We tiptoed across the field, beside the wood on our right, as far as possible from the house.

We had almost reached the end of the field, and the house was below, when I swore I glimpsed a Shape flitting between the tree trunks beside us. I froze and pointed. The others looked, said nothing. We shrugged, and continued; but we moved faster and faster, led by our gallant Chief of Staff. Then: a Howl. A long, low howl. Lord.... And worse – other long low howls; from all sides, it seemed. Very soft, hairily menacing, howls.

'I think', said the Doctor, moving forward faster, 'we had better get out of this.' 'A good job', gasped the Apprentice moving even faster, 'that Ulfsen doesn't like dogs....'

We panted uphill into the dark, followed, we swore, by Ulfsen's pet aversions.

Tree after tree silently slipped below us; we were gaining height. But so were They. Howls, sobs, moans, kept pace with us, swift, swifter as we puffed and stumbled; we dared not use a torch. At the last tree before the bare open hill, with a hint of dawn beyond that black vanishing ridge far – too far – away, we spontaneously stopped, backs to its trunk. We stood breathless, strained eyes into the night.

At first we saw nothing, heard nothing but the paddings about us. And, Lord, the breathings. Then, paddings stopped; and whatever They were, they were watching. We became aware, horribly, of green eyes surrounding us. In pairs, each pair capping a deeper patch of darkness. Dogs.... Dogs.

'Ho, there, boy....' suggested the Doctor, uncertain how otherwise to introduce himself.

A sort of snarl; like slowly torn-off sandpaper.

'There, there; boy....' he continued, rather desperately.

Another snarl, on the right. On the left, a long howl. The Apprentice examined the trunk for boughs. It was, mercifully, an old Scots pine not a Sitka, and we could – if threatened – leap and scramble up.

It was growing lighter; and our mouths dried with what we gradually saw. A whole pack of dogs encircled us, some staring at us, forefeet splayed, heads down; some sitting on their haunches, gazing at us with Red Indian gravity; others stretched out, regarding us chin on paw. Huge dogs, long grey dogs, curious sleekit hunting kind of dogs.

It was the Apprentice who voiced our mounting horror.

'Dogs! They're not bloody dogs: they're bloody WOLVES...!'

Wolves!

We leapt and scrambled furiously, chimps up a tree. I regret that I trod on the Doctor's face on the way up, but Nature is red in tooth and claw, and I needed a foothold just there.

On the third branch, we sat and considered the next move. Our General was clearly nonplussed. Still, Scipio Africanus eventually overcame Hannibal's elephants. We surely could out-manoeuvre Ulfsen's wolves.

But we did not. They came right up to the trunk, jumping and slavering, moaning and howling dreadfully. Hell of a row. The only consolation was that they never bared their teeth. 'Perhaps it's just play, perhaps they're quite friendly,' hoped the Doctor. But he was unwilling to test the assumption.

By eight o'clock we were sore and stiff but fairly familiar with the social habits of hungry wolves. Their sudden cessation of howling therefore aroused our interest. The Leader, then his Deputy, loped off; the remainder followed, leaving only a handful (*sic*) on guard beneath our tree. We were plotting, monkey-like, how to demoralise these obviously reluctant picketers when they began to howl again, noses skyward; and were answered by the others, evidently coming back. Our curses died in our mouths: accompanying the returning wolves appeared two men. Men – walking contentedly amongst them. One – a huge blond bear of a fellow in sandals – was actually roaring with laughter. He came and stood beneath our tree, slapping its trunk with one great pink hand and twiddling the Leader's ears with the other.

'Zo! You meet my vrens! Eh?'

We could not but agree.

'Kom on town, sey are harmless, harmless! Aren't you harmless, eh?' – this to the 'vrens'; the Deputy-Leader wriggled, all grisly two metres (it seemed) of him, with delirious acquiescence. We descended. Embarrassment is too mild a term for our scarlet confusion. But at least we had remained undevoured.

'They are... ah... fine animals,' volunteered the Doctor, unhappily.

'Vine – of course sey are vine. Sey are Vine Animals – but for von sing, von sing...' and he prised open the Deputy-Leader's jaws (the Leader being above such demonstration) – 'Look – sey haf NO TEES! NO TEES!

Indeed they had not. No teeth. None of them. And they set up a low wailing, as if lamenting that unfortunate (for themselves) absence. Ourselves, we felt immeasurably better. The Doctor cautiously tweaked a passing ear; its owner bared up at him a yearning demilitarised gum.

The other man had reappeared with a Land Rover and trailer. Out of the trailer he poured gallons of mash into troughs. 'Zee, ve veed sem here – for you! Sey vill not kom to seir eading place – zo! ve bring seir vood to sem. Sey vould not leaf you: sey are vond of you! Ho, ho, ho!' And he roared again, beating the tree till needles rained about us.

This was obviously Ulfsen. After introductions, he explained a little further.

'I am vond of Vulfs. My name it is Ulfsen, vich I zay means Zon of se Vulf.' He beat, this time, his own chest. A few wolves looked up from their troughs and growled agreement. 'Zo, I like keep vulfs all round me. But – ,' he leaned down at us, brows knitted (he was even taller than the Doctor, and three times as huge) 'I cannot keep vulfs in Zkottland – sey zay sey vill ead se TOURISTS!' – a great shout of laughter, in which we feebly joined – 'and zo, zo – I get sis Shenetic Breed of TOOSELESS VULFS! TOOSELESS VULFS! Sey vill not ead anybody!'

Toothless Wolves. All his fenced land was running with Toothless Wolves, that rare inbred strain from some Scandinavian genetics institute. We marvelled. We felt small. A Night Assault was nothing to this.

'Now – ' he darkened – 'tell me sis; vot vere you toing on my lant? In se night.... EH?'

We left it to the Doctor to explain. Which he did, admirably, with much Svensk lore, ancient and modern, thrown in; and a great friend of his at the Karolinska happened (naturally) to have treated Ulfsen's cousin for some condition as rare as that of his own wolves.... So all was well, very well. We drove down to a splendid breakfast ('NOW I ead se Zkottisk bregvazt, zee?') and were then accompanied by Ulfsen up the ridge to the very summit of Meall nam Fiaclan. He was enormously interested in Munros, Munroists and the story of Sir Hugh ('But I do not like your real glimbing – too dansherous – I like my vulfs!'). He would set aside a Route, a wide, wide Clearway 'up se rogs right to se Topp' himself: 'Sen, many many people can go!' But it was not all on his land? 'Pooh, pooh, it is von mountain. Only my vulfs I haf to keep in se vire.' And he brought us down to supper and fierce Skansk refreshments.

We asked him if it was really true he did not like dogs. 'Togs? Togs vorry my vulfs. Sey haf tees. My vulfs sey haf NO tees. Sat is not VAIR? Eh? Zo I zay – NO TOGS!' And he handed us another Finnish aperitif, some three to four degrees above Absolute Zero.

Yes, a very satisfactory ending.

And all this fuss about Access? Well, clearly, there is no difficulty of Access which is not readily resolvable through an appropriately adult approach.

A RESCUE

'This is worse than Princes Street the day before the Festival. Or Zero Gully at Easter.'

It was. We were pushed, jostled, poked, stood on. People overtook us, some very rudely. We overtook others, more rudely still. Children and the aged dithered in front, were helped aside, were cursed at. Luggage dented us. Infants hooted and howled. We kept losing each other in the turmoil. A few fanatics even fought against us the other way, pale with exhausted hate.

We seized a rare opportunity when we were all together, and ducked to the left, under an overhang. Traffic thundered above us, turf and small stones trebled past us, the odd whispering sweetiepaper see-sawed beyond us 2000 feet to the A82. Aah.... Relax.... Stretch....

It was the Aonach Eagach on a fine day in late summer, and we had gone there for Doctorial 'old times' sake'; for a simple scenic stroll after the Apprentice had shown us, the previous day, some of the latest things across the glen. It was certainly a ridge of high pressure; we hoped it would remain unbroken.

'We'll wait here till sunset', declared the Apprentice, 'when the pubs are open and they've all gone home.' Otherwise, he'd be up for man-slaughter; simply walking on, he'd knock dozens off, either side: satis-fying, but morally wrong. The Doctor's suggestion of a descent by The Chancellor ('It's a good route, for 1920.') met with an expected response: equally morally wrong, much less satisfying. One ecological expedition sufficed for one day. Anyway, every gully would be pattern-bombed by these remorseless squadrons. We would wait. It was a fine afternoon.

At least you did see people. Fascinating. We clambered up our overhang and surveyed the procession. Occasionally friends appeared but were borne away by the current, their greetings submerged. Many parties were roped up, often only a few feet apart, lurid in astronauts' anoraks, tintinnabulating with promenade ironware; so the tanglement at times became epic. One of the helicopters droning above would have been useful in traffic control. Our detached and lofty superiority pro-voked, though, occasional misinterpretation. 'Are you stuck? Can we give you a hand?' called out one eager Youth Leader from the van of his bright-faced progeny. It was left to the more genial Doctor to smile him on, dismissively. Little did we know.

As the sun went down, so did most of them, and we were about to resume our nostalgic traverse when an agitated figure approached from the west, swinging and jumping through the slap-happy pinnacles.

'It's Sandy Oliphant!' cried the Doctor, 'Without babies, for once, or kids of any kind. Never sampled pure undiluted 35-year-old Oliphant for ages.' We thought we'd recognised him earlier, chuffing among a steaming train of schoolchildren, acting as porter, guard, stoker and driver up and down the line.

He appeared in great distress. Had any fallen off? The Doctor pursed lips as Sandy panted nearer. 'Ridiculous, taking kids along a rotten ridge like this, with such exposure and no escape. Kids depend on us adults absolutely. We should be more careful. Sandy tends to overdo things.' We doubted if any single sprog would have been adept enough to push out of such a press, and fall. Probably a whole string had gone. Dreadful.

But no. Nobody had fallen. One, however, had decided to go home, his own way – 'home' being a camp down in the glen. He was sick of the queue. To Sandy's horror this independent youth had airily waved, jumped and slid down to that horrible loose south face. Despite entreaties he would not – probably could not – climb back up. When last visible, he was squatting on the edge of a gully, giving thumbs-up to his hand-wringing conductor – who, having noticed us a little way back, had tethered the others by a firm injunction to some rock, and then bolted here for help.

No, no, he didn't want official Rescue Teams just yet. The boy was intelligent ('Certainly is, getting out of this lot,' remarked the Apprentice) and would surely be waiting for assistance. 'You are the only competent climbers I've seen here,' gasped Sandy, 'You could nip over and get him up – or safely down – without any fuss. I daren't risk fuss, it would upset the others, scare the parents – and we've been that careful all weekend.... People talk so....' Sandy is totally without guile, and we were touched more than flattered. We bounded along behind him, towards his bereft and quivering flock.

'You know,' hissed the Doctor, 'he should have got the M.R.T. right away. Lord knows what that boy'll get up – or down – to. I don't like these private arrangements to save face, where kids are concerned – they're more important than anyone's pride.'

Of course, we had no rope or pegs. Not for a walk like this (it is indeed classified – by some – *as* a Walk....). Only a short nylon line – for emergency. We peered down. In the dusk a small figure crouched above the network of dilapidating overhanging gullies. Still there. Poor kid.

'Fine, we'll pop down and collect him. If we see a good way out, we'll take it. And signal by torch. Then you get the rest home and drive to the bottom and pick us up. Otherwise we'll have to try and climb back up this awful stuff.' Thus the Doctor.

A most unpleasant descent. The Doctor, skilled in horticultural psychology, led us through the less neurotic vegetation. My fingernails gathered *Graminaceae* and *Ericaceae*, the Apprentice no longer enjoyed what had promised to be the only interesting part of the day. 'All right, laddie, we're here!' cried the Doctor encouragingly, as he slithered down an invisible herbaceous thread among the unstrung and highly volatile vertical debris.

'So *you're* going this way, too?' the boy called up.

He was not shocked. Not alarmed. Rather, he seemed impatient. He finished what appeared to be sandwiches, rolled the paper into a ball and tossed it into horrifying black depths. Then, waving cheerily, he vanished after it into the gloom. 'Come on, then, it's easy enough below!'

'Lord, the boy's a madman!' wailed the Doctor, and literally shinned down the ghastly slope. 'He can certainly climb – downwards, anyway.'

We caught him up, at the top of another gut-rocking gully. 'I think this'll go all right', he was saying. The Doctor clutched him, none too gently. 'Careful!' exclaimed the boy, with annoyance, 'If you're going to slip, tell me first. Don't grab!'

We tried to instil some sense of guilt. 'Don't you know we've been called out to rescue you? Don't you realise your selfishness has caused us to risk our lives? We should really have had the M.R.T. out by this time, to do it properly – with more people risking their lives – and all in the papers tomorrow!'

The Doctor's exhortations fell unheeded. The boy – he must have been eleven or twelve – was pointing out his choice of route to the Apprentice, who appeared to agree. It seemed possible: with the Apprentice for the rock, the Doctor for the botany, and our 50-foot nylon line for any Emergency. Preferable to returning up that wall of short-fuse shingle, all triggered to go off downhill. We signalled back with our (only) headlamp, and then laced the vociferously protesting youth into the line.

To soothe him, we explained he was now our Leader. He demanded, if so, to wear the headlamp. No, the last man needed it, and *he* was not going to be the last man: he was Leader. Together, we quickly developed a technique. We dangled him down stretch after stretch, until he would call up 'O.K. – you fellers can come now, I've sorted it.' Then one by one we would slither down to him. And off he went again, raring to go. It resembled sounding the lead, as we repeatedly cast him overboard to find bottom.

And it worked very well. Too well. Until the last pitch.

This appeared, in the by-now darkness, to be a dungeon. We had lowered ourselves optimistically – and apparently irreversibly – into it. Sheer walls, left, right, and – now – up in front of us. Our feeble headlamp (it was really only for Emergency...) scraped unhappily on the wet rocks, and on the impending vegetation behind us, most of which had been swept off beneath feet, shins, backsides and shoulderblades. Damn.

'Looks like some fun, here,' remarked the boy. He offered us a Polo mint each. 'Sorry I've no more to spare: didn't reckon on company, like. We might need the rest later,' he further informed us, sucking composedly. 'Now, shine a light, Doc; just let's have a look down there....' and wriggled off. Our expressions were fortunately blacked out. Minutes. Badger-rattlings beneath; pebbles echoing away below. Then a shout.

'Fine. Just right. Come on, I've got you.... Quite safe.' However, we proceeded cautiously. Everything was rotten, undoubtedly irreversible. The boy had been astonishingly lightfooted. Only his (the boy's) presumed innocence prevented the accustomed string of maledictions from the insecure and disapproving Apprentice.

We found ourselves in a wet pit at the bottom of the dungeon, where some 1500 feet of trickle congregated before agreeing to run out beside

our feet through a large narrow slot like a letter box. Out to freedom. We knelt in the gurgles and peered. The boy took our headlamp and demonstrated a flash of easy screes down to the road beyond this otherwise seemingly impossible chockstone.

'Terrific, eh?' He was pleased at having guided us to so elegant an exit. 'O.K.? I'll go on....' And he slipped through, tied to his line, wearing the headlamp. 'Now you fellers.'

In the blinding flash-back beam, the Apprentice tried first. Then myself. Then the Doctor, that usually infinitely extensible assemblage of limbs and stratagems. Groan. Curse. Rip.

The boy was most helpful and patient. 'Try breathing *out*, it reduces your chest,' he advised the Doctor, speechless within the Tertiary.

No. We all stuck. We could not get through. And because we had no other torch, and had forgotten crowbar and Semtex, there we would stay until it was light or until someone could climb up the outside tonight and toss us a rope from the top of the chockstone. We could hardly ask our Charge to do that – now that we had successfully brought him to safety....

'Ah; and I thought you'd be able to do it. Too bad,' sympathised the lad. 'After coming down so well, all that way.' A pause. 'Do you want me to arrange a Rescue, like?'

'He is mature for his years,' gritted the embittered Doctor, with professional self-control. 'No!' he shouted, 'just tell Sandy about it. He's coming up the road. He'll know what to do. Don't make a fuss, under any circumstances. No need to disturb people at this time of night.'

The lad came back and hissed through the slot. His beam danced on our feet, wickedly.

'No, we don't want any more people risking their lives. Just selfish. And it'd be in the papers, tomorrow, like. Though the M.R.T. *would* do it properly....' He stopped. The Apprentice had partially blown a safety valve. 'O.K.' he resumed, 'I'll no rescue you, then: if you'll no rescue me – see? Fair do's, eh?'

'Fair do's,' replied the Doctor slowly. It was checkmate. 'Be careful, now,' he added feebly, as the boy whistled off and darkness became total, our line – still tied to the brat – slipping through nerveless hands. 'Let him keep it – it'll be safer, with him going down alone....' The Doctor sighed. A private arrangement, not the M.R.T. thank heaven.

For, this time, children were not *really* concerned.

Our child certainly wasn't. We heard him whooping away in sprays of scree. A most competent youth. He would be Minister of Sport yet. And at least he had given us a mint each.

Agonies of hunger, cold and wetness were nothing to the thought of the headlines and our colleagues' mirth if that urchin failed to keep his word. 'Boy Aged 11 Brings Three Experienced Climbers Down Safely.' 'Young Child Rescues His Instructors in Glencoe Mountain Drama.' 'Wee Hero....' Lord, they would pay him thousands....

Twice the Apprentice tried, twice he fell back, accompanied by his holds. Useless in the dark. Better to walk down in shame than be carried.

We must have dozed, for a light woke us. A voice. Sandy's, thank the Lord. Beside us.

'How did you get in here?' we asked, seeing no rope.

'Through the little keyhole up there on the left....' and Sandy pointed his beam. 'You can really only see it from outside. The boy described it to me. He left cairns to guide us, the whole way up.' So he did know of an easy way out, all the time.... our respect for the creature grew even greater.

As we stumbled to the road, munching chocolate bars, Sandy and his friend, a lean sardonic schoolteacher who, it appeared later, had suffered much from pontificating mountaineers, explained that the boy had stopped their car and told them.

'Has he... has he told anyone else?' we mumbled.

The schoolteacher whistled an unpleasing tune and kicked the odd stone.

'Don't think so. He went straight to bed,' said Sandy.

'Probably had a pint first,' scowled the Apprentice, all of an inch high.

'I didn't scold him,' explained Sandy. 'From what he told me, I gathered you wouldn't have liked us to.' Gulp. 'He's a curious child', Sandy continued, 'unexpectedly adult in so many ways. But unpredictable, quite unpredictable.' We shivered. 'I don't think I shall bring him again. He puts a great strain on everybody, you know.' We knew.

Our own great strain lasted more than a fortnight. We avoided radio bulletins and newspapers. We escaped possible journalists. Eventually we breathed. And now – now – we can even recount it; or much of it.

'A most extraordinarily well-balanced young person – in every sense,' summed up the Doctor, admiringly – also, thankfully. 'And, remarkable, isn't it – we never asked – we don't even know his name!'

The Apprentice put it more truthfully.

'Don't want to know his bloody name....'

POSTSCRIPT: But we nearly found out his name. Some Thursdays later, the *Journal* New Climbs Editor strode into the back bar of Daddy McKay's and flung a piece of paper down in front of us. 'What's all this nonsense?' he cried, 'here's a fellow done a quite unnecessary route off the Aonach Eagach, and says he led *you* down it, and *you* will vouch for it being a fine lead, a fine route, and well worth publishing....' We paled, and read. Yes, we recognised the pitches; the last one 'goes through a horizontal cleft to easy screes and the main road; the corpulent, aged or stiff avoid it by a traverse up and left....' 'Of course, I'll not publish it. The fellow has the cheek to say if I don't he'll send a much fuller version elsewhere. Good luck to him, then!'

We froze.

'Er, well, it's – er – after all quite an *interesting* way off', mumbled the Doctor, 'unforgettable, in fact. Do be a good chap, and put it in, this once....'

It took a great deal of Glen Droolie to convince the editor, but finally we breathed again. Before he left, we glanced hurriedly at the name of the climb; but never dared – then or later in the *Journal* – to read the name of our leader.

'I see he calls it *A Gentle Squeeze*....' mused the Doctor.

'His letter says it could be called *Blackmail*, but he thinks you'd agree that *A Gentle Squeeze* would look better, if it were printed in the *Journal*.'

When we were on our own again, we swore long and softly.

'Unexpectedly adult in so many ways,' sighed the Doctor. And drowned the whole juvenile episode in a truly mature Glen Droolie.

B GULLY

We shall leave it as B Gully, and not name the hill it defaces. To say more would endanger the innocently curious; few people would otherwise find it, and only the Doctor would look for it. What it does in summer I don't know, and don't care. It probably breeds rabbits. In winter it drives one to theosophy or astrophysics.

That New Year the Apprentice, the Doctor and I had gathered some excellent high grades in the Western Cairngorms. The Apprentice found them relaxing after two days with the Weasels, wintering summer VS's on the Ben. The Doctor, no mean performer on ice, had led several hard pitches and was high for the last day. However, the night before, it blew and snowed so arctically that we resolved to go home. But the morning radio reported no road at Dalnaspidal or anywhere else; so we resigned ourselves agreeably to an extra day's climbing. But where?

The southeast wind had filled all the northerly gullies and they lay together in the cold morning sun hatching powder-snow avalanches, joining wicked hands and waiting for us. We turned to the less intelligent hills opposite, a huddle of bent and balding brows.

'That wind should have cleaned out Beinn X', pronounced the Doctor (naming the unmentionable hill) 'and both its gullies. I read somewhere that B Gully is an easy snow walk with fine views south. We could have a gentlemanly stroll up it and watch for the ploughs coming through.'

We were not enthusiastic. But he had been robbed of a final good lead; so we assented. Beinn X was blunt bad-tempered scree, a dreadful slagheap of windblasted icy detritus; yet its two distant gullies blinked harmlessly enough. We headed for B Gully, through snow-dispensing Sitka spruce. 'Still,' remarked the Doctor, when we thankfully broke clear, 'they add a touch of difficulty to an otherwise easy day' – his usual, and usually accepted, invitation to Fate. We wiped our necks dry and followed a welcome path past a shepherd's cottage to the hill itself.

The gully began mildly enough. Its snow was hard and its angle slight. The jaundiced eye did note, a little way up, the whiter whiteness of deep new snow. The Doctor disagreed. 'Never, in a wind like last night's. All the loose stuff's been blown to Lochaber. Look how there's none on the scree.' He was still enlarging upon this certainty when he began to diminish. He was progressively entering his footsteps. We waded after, cursing his bobbing head. We were climbing into, not up, the gully.

'Don't worry. A softish patch. A mere aeolian aberration – due to that big rock – ' and he waved his axe towards the uniform scree slope on our right, which faced the equally uniform one on our left. 'We'll soon strike bottom again.'

And he ploughed on, treadmilling determinedly. No bottom could we strike. It was wrapped in eiderdown. We climbed through an endless sleeping bag. The floor could be stamped to some quiver of stability; front and sides fled from our grasp, and fell in again behind. Loyally, we underwent an hour or so of this. The Doctor, ahead in the burrow, kept promising an eventual excellent view of the snowploughs; an inducement we considered insufficient and, increasingly, improbable.

Then a mist came up from the strath; and our floundering lost any trace of relevance. We were isolated in space, each performing a private inexplicable penance. Up, down; up, down. Down, up; down, up. _Om mane padme hum._

Nothing could we see but occasional toiling pieces of ourselves. The environment had abdicated. Its ghost hung around in a thick flannel of expectancy. No doubt some Beatitude was preparing. Sensory deprivation is, however, unsuited to the impure, and our unemployed reflexes became restive. We spoke to them severely. But they prevailed. Nirvana would have to wait.

'I've had enough of this bloody place,' roared the head, shoulders and one arm of the Apprentice. Another arm, ectoplasmically dim, floated above him in vague Blavatskian deprecation; it repeated the Doctor's familiar assurances that rock would soon appear and that the view would be good. It withdrew and faded, exorcised by pulverising oaths from a demi-head sable, couped at the neck, issuant from an infinite field of argent.

Beinn X is only two and a half thousand feet at the worst, but to continue would disperse ourselves further into a dubiously-heraldic spirit world. B Gully under these conditions – probably under any conditions – is not the Eightfold Noble Path. It was not any sort of path; and to descend proved as baffling as trying to go up. Merely to stand still in such a whiteout entails much geometric unhappiness; the dimensions crowd round and leer unpredictably. They push back from in front and shove from behind. You inevitably fall. Our drunken progress down a thousand odd feet of this non-Euclidian picketing may be imagined.

We tried occasionally to escape from the side. During one of these time-consuming excursions the Doctor sang triumphantly 'A rock! A rock! At last! We're there!' And he carefully stepped on a small black triangle and pushed himself upwards. Then we knelt and pulled him out. He had stood on his own glove, dropped the moment before. The glove had, of course, vanished for ever into nether whiteness. We spat out snow and continued. B Gully had no sides any more; they had slipped, like the rest of our once so solid and Newtonian Beinn X, into a boundless continuum of uncertainty.

It was, in fact, impossible to measure advance in any direction. We began to sympathise with Einstein. The compass, and the Doctor's much-consulted but equally equivocal clinometer, tended to believe we were going down: yet small objects (borrowed from one's companion), when thrown ahead to prove this, would stick in mid-air; or annihilate themselves suddenly and permanently despite apologies. The Doctor aimed bearings from behind; but they never reached us. He blamed the Heisenberg principle. We suffered, in fact, most of the New Cosmology. Only a Black Hole was missing. It came later.

We swore we *were* going down. The air felt more still, and last night's snow-meringues loomed increasingly confectious. We became convinced we were descending a steep, sheltered and previously unseen branch of B Gully. Such unexpected fluvio-glacial gorges ferret these lower hills. We roped up and followed the Apprentice's erratic thread through piled hallucinations. The Doctor, at times disconcertingly below us, acted as anchor; he was our longest peg. But no steep pitch fell away beneath; whenever we imagined one, the Apprentice's torso would surmount it into space, a rising kite tight in our fingers.

It grew dark; but still no communication from Scotland. We leant against each other. We were light-headed from weltering in abstraction; our hemispheres had drifted up. We argued about the existence of torches; each assumed somebody else had brought one (only a gentle-manly stroll...). We would have to bivouac until this hopeless mist cleared up. The Apprentice, cursing dully, plunged his fist into the wall of snow before him to test its howff-forming potentiality.

His howls and fragmentary dance testified the negative. Solid. Obvi-ously ice. We had struck it at last. We *were* in a gorge. At a steep part. The ice appeared to rise above us; therefore it presumably stretched below. We collected ourselves. We smelt avalanches. I gathered the rope, and the Doctor, hovering beyond my shoulder, divested himself of legs and dug in. The Apprentice leant forward, sniffing cautiously, tapping with the point of his axe. Suddenly there was a thump and a dull crack, and a black line appeared across part of the wall; a fringe of dislodged snow trickled down it. Windslab! Windslab and powder snow.... This, then, was it.

'She's going!' croaked the Apprentice, snatching back his axe. The Doctor drove himself in, together with his comment, up to the hilt, and vanished from sight. I hauled on the rope and fell back into feathers, feet plunging. The Apprentice, as he later described it, was plucked from his steps and flung outwards and upwards....

We wrestled, clutching the rope, our only reality. It clutched back. Blows demolished my breath – we were over the wall – or was it the Doctor's boots? A rush of silence.... I imagined myself falling, falling, in the caress of a powder-snow avalanche, towards rocks or suffocation.

Then it seemed as if I awoke.

'Good Lord,' said the Doctor, just above my ear.

I clawed away snow. I felt myself carefully. Surprisingly, I could sit up, though it was painful.

We must have stopped; but we might never have moved. In front was an apparently identical ice wall, again with a black split across it. But the creaking and tearing was louder this time, and the split wid-ened, jerk after jerk. We heard tinkling, as of ice, into the abyss beyond. We were about to be swept down the next step of this appalling stair-way. We grabbed the rope again; and waited.

But the split grew wider, until it was almost a regular square. A black square. Our long-bleached eyes drank it with fascination. Black. Square. Hypnotised, we wrapped the rope round our arms.

And then, incredibly, the square slowly filled itself; and presented us

– with a Human Head. A large human – hairy and whiskered – head gazed at us from the square. Its eyes glittered in the half-light.

I groaned. This was Concussion; or worse. Maybe, The Other Side. Letting go the rope with one hand, I rubbed snow round my eyes. It was still there. 'Good Lord....' repeated the Doctor, perhaps appropriately.

The head spoke. With deliberation.

'Ye'll be the fellies: that went up the hill the day?'

Silence. 'Aah,' replied the Doctor, the only one with a biddable larynx.

'Well, then: jist ye come roon to the door: an I'll let ye in. It's awfy deep-like: oot there at the back. Wait now: till I pit on the licht.'

The head withdrew, and almost at once the square blazed forth. *Fiat lux*. It was not St. Peter. It was not The Gate. It was not even a Black Hole. It was somebody in a cottage. The cottage was snowed up at the back, it was whitewashed and, as the Apprentice had painfully demonstrated, it was built of sound local granite. There had been no avalanche, and we had fallen only in our own estimation.

We rose and followed the rope to the Apprentice, who had been buried and half strangled by our earlier presence of mind; pulled him up, brushed him down, stifled his questions and propelled him towards the approaching torch.

'Come awa in: come awa in. I jist couldna get yon windy open: an noo the gless is creckit. Pieces aa owre the flair. Michty: where hae ye been? Aa snaw? Ye've come doon the burn: that's what ye've done: richt aff the hill. But: ye'd like no *see* the road.'

We dripped beside a roaring fire, clutching hot sweet tea and new-made bread. Frying hissed wonderfully behind us. We gathered that there were only two places on the hill where snow always collected, B Gully and the burn that ran down from it directly to the shepherd's cottage, the cottage we had passed that morning. The burn, it seemed, was the usual place to find the more stupid sheep in weather like this.

'But: I've niver had three o them: at ma back windy afore!' exclaimed the shepherd, genially enough, pouring out drams for each of us.

We thought it best not to comment. Later, perhaps, the Doctor might describe how he had steered us straight to supper. Just now, he studied his whisky. We had begun hesitantly to discuss the hazards of lambing, when the shepherd's wife called us to table. Plates steamed, chips stretched themselves expansively on top of bacon, sausage and egg. 'And so it's Mr McPhedran you're knowing,' she said, naming the shepherd who had been our host on the Craggie expedition. 'He marches with us. A great man, Erchie, a great man.'

'Remarkable, remarkable, *mmm*, his fiddle has, *mmm*, exceptional bite and drive,' agreed the Doctor, munching affably, wielding his fork; and conversation was launched down the channel so tactfully provided.

ONE HITCH AFTER ANOTHER

'Nearly there!' shouted up the Doctor, with relief.

We were on a newish line of the Apprentice's, threading the west (worst) side of central Buttress in Coire Mhic Fhearchair. Not really new – it owed much to the Nisbetry sprinkled around; we had urged, cajoled and threatened our leader away from his original extremist aspirations. Especially as the weather had suddenly turned bad.

Very bad. Just as we reached the quartzite. Hellish, for July and July clothing. Long waves of hail, liquid and solid, howled from the north and broke against our cliff, numbing fingers and necks. We were soaked and cold. Below, wet glaciers slid off the Doctor's hat down each side of his nose. The Apprentice, invisible above, spat high-calorie expletives into the roaring freeze-for-all.

Jerk on the rope. My move. I grabbed and sliddered on rock uncooperative as ice. Sleet lubricated hailstone-bearings. This last pitch was just Severe technically but Extreme climatically....

It had been a superb lead. When we finally hauled in the long lobster legs of the Doctor through the top surf, we crouched shipwrecked on a bouldery summit shore.

'Too much windchill to face this lot back to the car,' gasped our Medical Adviser, wiping a streaming blue beak. 'Let's go over the ridge and down to the Glen Torridon road. Easily get a lift this time of year.'

The old Merc reposed due north at the foot of Glen Grudie. We peered that way. Sleet.... Howl.... Drench.... Visibility – nil. No question – due south over the ridge! Easily get a lift.... Up Glen Torridon, turn left at Kinlochewe and down to Glen Grudie. It was the way to Inverewe, taken by all the National Trusters – even in this weather, for it would be fine at the coast.

Out of the wind we became merely wet. Above us screamed horizontal plates of meteorology. We slid and spattered down to the innocent wet ribbon of road. We shook ourselves. We looked guilty and disreputable. So, as Front Man, we chose the more amiable Doctor, who – on a drippingly close examination – seemed to boast a clean shirt. He stationed himself, rucksack carefully minimised, by the sodden verge, sucking a drowned pipe, thumb poised as if to confer some imperial favour. We lower orders tried our luck downstream, ready to dash back – with armfuls of rope and pitons – to gaff whatever the Doctor had hooked. Three or four vessels splashed past every minute, bolted and shuttered as submarines, windscreen wipers in nervous frenzy. None stopped.

'It's not all that bloody far; better walk it than freeze here....' The Apprentice's opinion had barely been launched into the flood before a small one took the Doctor's bait. The near door opened. Rubbish was ejected. The Doctor inserted his beak.

We galloped down. A packed and steaming interior. Large elderly beaming occupants, eating. The driver leaned across ample Lancastrian bosoms and pastry.

'Ee, but you're wet!' We were. (Chew, chew).

'There's only room for one of you.' There was. (Chew).

But the Doctor could whizz up with them, collect the Merc and then collect us. He wiped his cascading neb once more and was about to squeeze in among the festal boards, when the Apprentice's ever-casting thumb caught a large empty BMW object.

Much better (we thought). We thanked the masticators and leapt to luxury and the proprietorial Apprentice – 'Just put the luggage in the boot.'

Brrrmm... Brrrmm... The driver, Billy, a large blue-eyed optimist, threw a fag-end out of his window. He wasn't going down Glen Grudie way, but Kinlochewe would do for starters, eh? Yes, yes. We could get a lift to Glen Grudie from there.

Yes. We crouched in horror at the take-off. He certainly thought he could drive. Radar is a wonderful thing – without it we could only see through eighteen inches of the wiper's arc; tourists – both ways – were devoured unseen. The infamous BMW back-end swivelled excitedly at every yank of the wheel. We clutched our belays.

Then a mate of his in some other thunderous aquatic monster (probably a Cosworth Ford) beat on our tail. Billy smirked and pushed his foot further down. 'Poor old Chairlie. He'll no get past, eh? Eh?'

Above the neurone-quelling CD six-speaker stereo-pop, Billy queried the sanity of our late sport. As for him, he was up here on a construction job. That made sense. But climbing – 'Jist no bliddy safe, thae hills. An in this weather, plain daft. Ach, ye ——— !!' (A Metro or suchlike had ventured too far from the gutter and fled back crying). 'Na, na. No me,' he bellowed cheerfully, eyes feeding on the rear mirror, 'Ah'll stay put. Terror bliddy firmer fer me! Eh?' He burst into loud song as we skidded the next bend, and lit another fag.

We were too stricken to peer through the gale-splashed glass. Another shuddering power-slide and we swung right, the great baying brute that had tried to overtake us having to brake hard alongside and vanish backwards to tuneful blasts of a seven-fold trumpet. We belted along, unchallenged.

'That was Chairlie. Cannae corner. Nae use. Ye have tae DRIVE on these roads: eh?'

The Apprentice took courage and rubbed his fist on the glass. He peered through. He yelled. That had not only been Chairlie, but Kinlochewe and our turn left.... We were almost halfway up Glen Docherty already, heading for Inverness, swinging furiously curve to curve, Chairlie way behind.

Eventually, with extremely bad grace, Billy slowed down to let us out. We leapt away as all gears gathered themselves and rear wheels sprayed.

It was off, leaving a creamy wake – with our kit still in the boot!

We roared in fury. The Doctor, perspicacious as ever, jumped into the road and flagged down Chairlie. We tumbled in, and urged him on. Faster, faster....

Nae use. Chairlie couldnae corner. We bumped from verge to verge in a frenzy of pursuit, cursing ditherers. Ye hae tae DRIVE on these roads.

Then, wonderfully, a queue ahead: sheep blocking the way. We slithered up to the savagely-revving BM, leapt out, beat the boot, tore it open and grabbed our things as – once more – wheels showered us and it stormed off. Chairlie trumpeted his derision, Billy shook a friendly fist out of the window and they roared away, foam to foam, overtaking joyously.

We collapsed, exhausted. We were so shaken we stopped the next car going up to Inverness, instead of down to Kinlochewe, and became lengthily entangled in broken European with the French occupants, who took us for Germans forgetfully signalling on the wrong side of the road....

We wearily waded to the opposite bank, and resumed supplication. A top-heavy launch-like campavan teetered unsteadily to stop beside us, stalling the engine.

A door slid back. Dozens of heads, mostly infantile, peered out.

'I can only take one,' warned a voice from way back. 'I'm not really used to driving this thing. We're full enough – we've had some near squeaks already.'

Despite this uninviting invitation the Doctor, a man of steel, stepped forward, cast a last glance at us and pulled up on the handle.

A muffled cry within, a horrid gurgle and splash, and he retreated hastily, slapping himself down. More cries.

'Ally's been sick again, Dad!' Rags were brandished from the doorway, showering us.

We staggered back, rinsed by the rain. No, we wouldn't inconvenience them further. We thanked them for the opportunity, and hoped Ally would get well. We ploughed on. We sighed for Central Buttress again. Elemental simplicity. Do or die. We could cope with that. But here – what were we doing here, sponging off everything we climbed away from each weekend? Were we really no better than anyone else? We were depressed. We were suffering from Severe Social Exposure.

Fortunately, another vehicle stopped beside us. (The weather was so dreadful, the stoniest heart would dissolve). Fortunately? It was a bulbous bluebottle-like Japanese pickup, with rusty cowcatchers, stone-guards, aerials, swivelling lights and a few canisters of – apparently creosote – in the open back.

The cabin was thick with joviality and fag smoke. Its window wound down and fresh air fled terrified.

'Aye, we're gaun to the Gairloch. That's your way. Chust chump in!'

We clambered into the back as it chuffed off in clouds of carbon. I grabbed the Apprentice – his hold had come loose; it clattered on the road behind us.

The Doctor lay on cold wet steel, feet outstretched against a canister. The Apprentice jammed his barrel into the small of his back. I embraced mine.

To little effect. All of them bounced and rolled and spat vile oily liquid at every bend. Black bilge sluiced our backsides.

But not far to go....

Hell once more! They turned back to Glen Torridon at Kinlochewe! They were *not* going down to Grudie! This was the same damned road we'd started off from....

We beat fists on the cabin roof, kicked it, wept and swore. The Apprentice sawed his canister to and fro across the cabin's back window bars. But they were too intent on some tattered tabloid inside, driver included.

At length they suspected something. They stopped suddenly and bashed open a door. (The Doctor, who was attempting a traverse along it to shout through a window, was dislodged instantly into the ditch).

Puzzled faces looked out, down, and up.

'You boys not well or something, is it? You'll be having the Car Sickness maybe?' (We certainly were, by now).

We spluttered that this was not the way to Gairloch, still less to Glen Grudie.

'Och, that's all it is, is it? Och, we've chust to pick something up at Inveralligin – a few drums of oil and stuff. It'll no take long, an hour or so. Inveralligin's a great place. Grand views in good weather. Then we'll chust come back and hit straight for Glen Grudie; you'll be home in no time, boys!'

Despite the risk of wounding their feelings, we stiffly dropped down to the Doctor in the rushes. They billowed off, genially distributing hydrocarbons.

The Apprentice swore he'd walk. WALK. We were a few hundred yards further *down* the road than when we started. We were not even holding our own.

So we splashed on, soaked, clapped out, smelly.

Then just before the Ling hut a big shiny car stopped beside us. And offered a lift. Opened doors and urged us in, despite our understandable hesitation. It was so warm, dry and clean. Hospitable old Yorkshire couple. The wifie leaned back as we melted into the rear seat.

'My, you *are* wet. It's all that *rain*, that's what it is!'

Yes, the driver said yes, they were going to, to Inverewe.

'Inver, Inversomething, isn't it, Doris, we're making for?' Much fumbling about a road atlas, and ultimate agreement. Direct to Glen Grudie at last....

'We'll not get to Inver, Inverwhatsitsname today, but you say it's on your way, so just tell us when you want to get off.'

We sighed and relaxed. It was warm, dry and soft. And slow.

Lord, it was slow. The driver, Ernest, was excessively careful. These dreadful roads were so dangerous. This dreadful weather was so dangerous. And these drivers were so dreadful, so dangerous. So fast, so rude, so thoughtless of Other People – always wanting to Overtake.

Ernest swivelled round – slowly and alarmingly – in his (driving...) seat and addressed us severely:

'I never let... 'em Overtake. I teach 'em... Manners.'

Yes, yes, we agreed agitatedly. Only turn round again, for the Lord's sake. We thought of Billy heading back for something he'd forgotten.

Ernest resumed his righteous peering through the flung monsoon. Hooters shrieked behind us incessantly. He veered out and kept 'em back. He checked his speedometer – 25 miles per hour. Fast enough in this weather. He taught 'em Manners.

Our ears burnt. Doris kept on knitting.

Surely we should have been warned, by this time. But it was warm, dry, and we daren't look out of the streaming windows with half a mile of accumulated fury behind us. Bellowings, bleatings, roars; like the dawn chorus at Perth Mart. And he was so slow.

'Listen to 'em. Mad. Always hootin. Always RACIN. They should enjoy the... Country. That's what it's for. It's not a... Speed Track. Is it, Doris?'

An evil dream. Unending. But warm. Then, in a brief comparative lull, we looked more closely out of the window.

No.... No! Glen Docherty! AGAIN! We had passed Kinlochewe and not turned left!

We were rude. We shouted. We pounded the back of the front seats.

Ernest appeared upset. 'But you did say... Inver, Inver, Inver... didn't you? That's where we're going, we turned right, at the sign.'

Doris put away her knitting slowly, and consulted navigational aids. She looked up, round-eyed, at Ernest.

'You know, I think it's Inver*ness* that we mean.' She turned worried lenses on us. 'Is it Inver*ness* you're going to, then?'

No! We continued to shout, shake and stamp. We continued to be assisted up Glen Docherty. Finally, on a blind corner, they stopped and let us out, shaking their heads. A cavalcade of blaring open-window-cursing vehicles ground past. We choked in the smoke of at-last-released exhausts.

'A bloody yo-yo!' screamed the Apprentice. He foamed. He was no longer depressed, but manic. He would much have preferred a decent honest death in Glen Grudie.

We shambled on down again. We were such poor drookit craiturs by then that a car stopped within two minutes. Gold specs, grey costumes. Three old ladies. National Trust, of course. Inverewe. Room for one. The Doctor hopped in. 'This is it! Soon be back! *Keep richt on Tae the end o the road...*,' he sang.   And vanished.

We two splashed on. A long pause. Then hot dieselly breath on our necks. A silver Range Rover, Edinburgh registration. An inviting door. We hauled ourselves in. Behind us wire mesh and two slobbering wolfhounds; in front, a tweedy lady and a kilted driver, Balmoral bonnet and all. The latter burbled forth.

'Jolly good! We're going along your way to Little Loch Broom. Delighted to help. So glad you're enjoying yourselves out here. Wonderful country. I like it best in this kind of... wildish weather, don't you? Sort of wind and rain on your face. Rather splendid for tramping about. Love to come up for a month or so in the summer. Kind of ancestral home, you know.' We recognised Ancient MacKenzie tartan and the plastic sprig of holly. The fruity R.P. vowels cantered on.

'My great grandfather sold his place up here and came to Surrey. And my grandmother was a Cameron – from Henley. So it's rather in the blood, you know. *Still the Heart is Highland* – even at Haslemere, hah!' We remarked on his number plate. 'Ah, I always have my cars registered in Scotland... keeps up the link, don't you see?' He blethered on compulsively. 'Now we're going to our daughter's – nice little place where she can paint and her husband can fish, watch birds and shoot 'em, and try to breed oysters. Of course he has his Fax to Lombard Street, keeps in touch with the necessary.'

His wife swivelled round and flashed a toothy explanation – 'Diana married a Bradbury-Hutton!'

We badly missed the Doctor, who would certainly have appeared to know all about Bradbury-Huttons and breeding oysters. Our monosyllabic answers were not only due to the Apprentice's black thoughts about White Settlers, but to our anxious watch for the old Merc pounding back up; we could easily miss it – on a day like this.... We were also melting like ice cream under the wolfhounds' plushy tongues, the netting being permeable to canine affection.

The Mhic Choinnich prattled on. He skilfully missed a beached cyclist baling out, and nearly ran over the legs of some poor subaquatic sod changing a wheel. Otherwise, an uneventful trip to the foot of Glen Grudie. As we climbed down, Himself reached under the steering wheel and his lady passed on to us a hip flask.

We were taken aback. Haslemere Hospitality. Embarrassed, I thought it appropriate to toast our nostalgic native with the MacKenzie war-cry: '*Tulach ard!*'

He appeared equally taken aback. 'Er, no, actually,' he said. 'Chevas Regal.'

Freed at last from our prolonged battle with the Knights of the Road, we strolled through fresh wet grass to the old Merc – still there, thank goodness. A few other cars, too. But no Doctor.

'He'll be in Inveralligin, admiring the view,' suggested the Apprentice. 'We'll leave a note on the seat and collect dry things for the tent.' (Tent – blessed secret sanctuary! There, snug at last from wind, hail, sleet,

Billys, Ernest and Lombard Street, we could celebrate again the warm sandstone and gleaming quartzite of our Central Buttress in the sun.)

We possessed no key. But my companion is suspiciously skilled at entering locked vehicles within the prescribed 12 seconds, and I admired the way he dismantled, with wire and a plastic card, the Doctor's ingenious booby-traps.

'Dead easy,' he proclaimed, loudly.

And then the roadside blossomed with figures.

'Hi! hi! You there!' 'Stop thief, stop thie-e-e-ef!'

We blinked. Many waterproofs, Barbour jackets and severe expressions closed in on us from their ambush. We were not yet done with our fellow men.

'Got you at last, you rats!' bellowed an unpleasantly large and powerful cove. 'Filthy swine!' screamed an emotional lady. 'You took my camera yesterday,' cried another. 'And my *best* binoculars,' squeaked a portly professional gentleman rotating a *Daily Telegraph* umbrella, 'the ones I brought for the Great Crested Grebe!' .

'The police will be here DIRECTLY!' triumphed the first lady. 'George has a phone in his car!'

The three largest characters attempted to clutch us. We had no intention of being clutched, and the Apprentice unslung ironmongery for this unexpected pitch. They halted, but all hope of a brawl faded when a white car purred to a halt on the road above and a lithe figure leapt out, saluted the occupants and strode down to us.

Our assailants, hopeful of police, gazed expectantly.

'Ah, got back before me after all,' cackled the Doctor benignly. 'We had a puncture. Damned wet job – and some fool nearly ran me over. But lucky I was there: the three old dears were quite helpless. But most generous' – he extended a large box of fine chocolates through the bucketing rain –

'Your friends like some, too?'

A SPONSORED WALK

I suppose we did ask for it. The previous day we had forced a rather extempore new line on Sgòran Dubh, between Bachelors' Buttress and Married Men's Buttress, which the Doctor wished to call Unwedded Bliss and the Apprentice, Birth Control. An unsavoury argument early next morning was resolved by the Doctor suddenly exclaiming:

'Lord! I promised to meet Sandy at Corrour Bothy this afternoon... He's there with his family: wife, and baby twins. You know', he added apologetically, 'they all go out together. He *does* that kind of thing....'

We were tied to the Doctor's transport at Derry Lodge that night, and Sandy Oliphant – though somewhat tiresome about birds, beasties, kiddie-widdies and other good causes – offered what then seemed a wholesome change of subject. We had reservations about babies – and sprogs generally – and Sandy Oliphant displayed a weakness for organising Young Folks' Festivals, Bairns' Bus-trips and so forth. His house rocked to merry cries over Hallowe'en and most of the year it clapped and cheered with Parties. We shuddered. 'But he won't have much scope at Corrour', the Doctor pointed out, 'and he'll be extra careful, with the babies: it's their first trip.' So we meekly followed him out of Glen Einich. It was our last day, anyhow.

In the hot sun we foolishly preferred to grind round the north end of the Lairig rather than grill over the tops.

We struck the track quite low down, above what had evidently been a vast recent encampment. Despite a memorably dry summer, the place was flattened in mud and the path a quagmire. Huge clarty holes; hundreds, thousands of scampering footprints.

We had long been wary of popular solitudes and the Lairig seemed as trampled as a Serengeti overspill. We gaily identified deep prints of wildebeest and striped ones of zebras. 'Migration,' explained the Doctor. 'Lots of people use it now; camping each end, and in the middle at Corrour. Those in Braemar want to get to Aviemore; those in Aviemore have a passion for Braemar. Perfectly natural. Other side of the fence. Like the three Tailors that New Year's Eve.' (They had danced a reel in Rothiemurchus and went on to dance one in Braemar; a stone on the hillside, *Clach nan Taillear*, marks their final set....)

More than three tailors made this mess. We pictured the hapless conservationists and path-restorers sweating with shovels, crowbars, creosoted beams and plastic netting, while helicopters sprayed hundredweights of Ecological Seed about them.

'Natural erosion,' averred the Doctor. 'Should be left to take its course. If it discourages people, so much the better; negative feedback. Dynamic ecosystem.'

'Positive bloody feedback,' objected the Apprentice, clambering out of one particularly unsavoury pothole, filled with the droppings of what seemed a hundred deer. We were argumentative that day, even in so peaceful a scene; which, after the flinty obliquities of the Buttress, appeared an oasis – a morass – of Innocence.

'Strangely quiet,' unwisely observed the Doctor.

A subdued twittering ahead grew louder. Then the Apprentice leapt back from the next hole, just at the summit. Three – not tailors but – little girls, climbed out the other side and waved him on.

'That's a bad one; but the next's *much* worse!' they informed him happily, plastered in mud. They wore summer shoes and dresses. Huge fun.

When we struggled out and joined them we could see far down the Lairig. 'My God!' exploded the Doctor, as near Aghast as I have know him.

There appeared an endless string of small children, smaller children, large ones, bobbing and dipping all the way down the astonished defile. Gesticulating taller figures galloped alongside, endeavouring to exhort, extract or admonish their charges. A bright bubbling of sound, as from a moorland burn, punctuated by agitated whaup-like whistles. Hundreds of 'em. Thousands.

'I told you we should have called it Birth Control,' said the Apprentice bitterly. 'I expect they're all going to see your Mr Oliphant....'

'Yes, we *are*! Are *you*?' cried one of the trio now trotting and jumping beside us, fuelled inexhaustibly by pocketfuls of Mars Bars and the like.

'*You're* going to see Sandy?' asked the Doctor in disbelief. 'Sandy Oliphant?'

'Oh, is that his name? What a lovely name! Maggie, Mr Oliphant's name's Sandy! Mister, what's Mrs Oliphant's name?'

'And the Baby Oliphants' names?' squeaked up the smallest and grubbiest, yanked along by Maggie. 'What's the Baby Oliphants' names?'

'Er, Betty... is his wife's; and... I don't remember those of the children....' stuttered the Doctor helplessly. He indicated the vociferous files in front: 'Are you *all* going to see the Oliphants?'

'Oh, yes, Oh yes, ALL of us! That's why we're here.'

'Gey popular family,' muttered the Apprentice. 'Do *we* have to go? I don't think they'd miss us,' he added.

Further enquiry elicited the whereabouts of the Oliphants, who acted as a communal Pied Piper for all the bunch. They were assembled down at the front, at a Camp, the second of three along the route. Yes, the whole family – the babies had curly hair, they were twins, it was their first trip. They'd brought everything with them – big, big sacks of food, buckets to wash with, trunks to carry things in.

'A bit overdoing it,' mused the Doctor. 'Even with two sprogs a couple of extra rucksacks should be enough. But Sandy never does things by halves. And there's all this mob. It'll be Corrour, as he said. I expect this is one of his Sponsored Walks. Good job the weather's fine.'

But *what* a mess. What a smell. They had churned up years of Cervid sewerage. 'Like a monkey house,' sniffed the Apprentice. We took to the braes above for easier going, and overtook rapidly.

An astonishing sight – as far as you could see, milling, billowing, bouncing heads. Around, above them, fluttering in the gentle July breeze, a myriad butterflies of sweetie papers.

The braes got rougher, so we ran alongside and pushed our way through. Scouts, Rovers, Guides, Boys' Brigadiers, all the Responsibles, barked up and down the plowtering lines, keeping everyone safe.

'There's three away at the very back: Maggie and pals,' the Doctor informed one hyper-active young citizen, who thanked him profusely and cantered rearward, dispersing the corries with his three-tone whistle.

We were now jammed, moving desperately slowly; they had overflowed both banks. Then we spied, perspiring past, be-ribboned with whistles and compasses, maps, first-aid and a walkie-talkie, none other than Evergreen Smith – it was, after all, his kind of circus. We heard Doggie encouraging him above even this racket, with frantic mud-entangled yapping somewhere among the feet.

The Doctor roared, and grabbed Evergreen – or, rather, slightly delayed him *en route.*

'Sandy Oliphant, Sandy Oliphant, is he at Corrour?'

Evergreen pulled free, trotting backwards at great hazard, patting small erratic heads and reassembling his cords and cables, sadly deranged by the Doctorial clutch. Before plunging away again he gasped out:

'Sandy? No, he's not here, the kids have got chicken-pox. They've *all* got chicken-pox....'

Not here. Chicken-pox. What the, how the...

'The Oliphants have got chicken-pox!' repeated the incredulous Doctor loudly, stopping dead and being pushed on again from behind. 'Did you hear that – the Oliphants have got *chicken-pox!*'

A long officious individual did hear this. He in turn grabbed the Doctor. His spectacles flashed alarm.

'Chicken-pox? Chicken-pox?'

'Yes, they've got chicken-pox. Just found out. Most unfortunate for the kids.'

The officious one's mouth opened. Then it clamped firmly on to a whistle, a really LOUD whistle, for he was an important man.

Blast! Blast! said the whistle.

Pandemonium. Some officials were still urging the procession on, others trying to hold it back, crying 'Chicken-pox, chicken-pox, the Oliphants have got chicken-pox! Everybody stand back, everybody stand back!'

We scrambled ashore and sat on a large stone to eat our pieces. The tide about us rose and fell. Flotsam was flung out, reabsorbed. Screams and tears. Fighting. Clawing. Most distressing – and quite, quite incomprehensible. Why the panic about chicken-pox when Sandy's crew wasn't even there? When it was lying bespotted somewhere in Edinburgh?

The sea had fallen to a sullen murmur and we elbowed, chewing the last crust, through its weeping mass – a damp distasteful progress – towards Corrour. At least *there* someone ought to know. More holes. Worse smells. Great lumps of deer dung. This was – or had been – Corrour meadow.

We peered through heads and arguments at the distant Bothy. Beside it were pitched four large igloo tents, two of them huge. Obviously for the Committee. They were festooned with guys and with things hung over them to dry. People milled about them. Someone actually scrambled up the largest one and sat unsteadily on its top. He waved his arms. Everybody waved their arms. Cheers above the lamentations.

A tremendous trumpet call. Another. Flags were brandished. Wild cheers.

As bad as the Queen's Birthday; a sort of Corrour Gathering.

Trumpets again. Paper streamers.

The tents shuggled.

Then they moved, and began walking away.

Walking away....

It dawned.

Elephants....

Not Oliphants.

Elephants. In the Lairig Ghru. I suppose we should have guessed. The Doctor was with us that day. Elephants in the . . . .

Of course, it took time. But eventually all were reassured. The elephants had not got chicken-pox. Everybody was safe. Maggie, Tottie & Co. met Sandy. Had a ride on him and on a baby with curly hair. It took time, and was very late, midsummer dark, before the mob was counted, fed and put into their tents; and before the elephants, feet bathed and now unbound from miles of safety bandage, had peace to pack helicopters-worth of hay into their trunks. But it was all for a Good Thing, this 'Operation Hannibal' (as the organisers christened it); for the R.S.P.C.A., P.D.S.A., Dogs' Homes, Cats' Homes, Birds' Homes. And they were tolerant, kindly beasts.

Not so the Apprentice, faced with a long dark walk to Derry Lodge, demanding in righteous rage who would pay for repairing the paths, who would pick up all the paper, who would thank heaven – most devoutly – that the weather had stayed fine, who the devil – he appealed to the very place where Auld Nick had made his point – had dreamed up such an earth-destroying, sprog-endangering, elephantastically crack-pated scheme...?

The Doctor sighed, and handed another snoring brat to an official.

'Sandy Oliphant, I expect. He does that kind of thing.'

CLIMBING AGAINST TIME

One by one we heaved ourselves over that most satisfying sun-warmed dolerite, and relaxed upon dry gravel and wet spring snow. We had made our own way to the top of a fine broken buttress; no particular route, just moderate mixed May mountaineering, ropeless and relaxed.

'You can't beat a simple off-piste line,' yawned the Doctor, stretching luxuriously before the wet seeped through, and ostentatiously pushing back the shingle with clinkered heels and gleaming tricounis. And certainly, on a climb like this, those nails (as the Apprentice and I had demonstrated every few cursing minutes) were much superior to our vibrams; we had left front-pointers in the car, for such a route in such weather would have meant either expensively blunting them or infuriatingly wooing them on and off our boots every couple of yards. 'A delightfully unconstrained few hours of exploration,' he purred, shifting to a dry patch and unwrapping the pieces, 'Just what the Old Boys did, in those gone-for-ever take-it-easy uncomplicated Golden Days. Wish we could join them for a bit. Too late now.'

We indulged him, for today was indeed a contrast. Our last meeting, two weekends before, had been in England, watching the Apprentice – as one of a team of Weasels – sweating through a highly-publicised highly-prized Sport-Climbing Competition in the Galactoramic All-Star Sports Hall at Grabsworth. He had done such things before, even at Bercy, but had kept his secret, as others hide their loot of Munros. Now, however, being expert (flashing a 5.12d) he had shyly asked us down to cheer him on. Which we did; though finding the whole performance somewhat odd. Through floodlights, spotlights, TV harnesses and an amplified rockfall from some incessantly detonated Group, we watched competitor after competitor assault the craftily-contrived wall. Its successive pitches billowed upwards in different colours, each one heliotropically advertising its own commercial sponsor. At the very top, above the overhang, it surged to silver, then gold.

A loud bell proclaimed the conquest of every crux, rising to electronic whoopee at the (very rare) final victorious few metres. Applause roared continuously, the commentator bellowed incoherently, figure after bronzed figure clad in lurid pants or imaginatively-stretched bikini sleuthed its way up by unbelievable exudations of strength, gymnastics and willpower. The Doctor especially enjoyed cheering the speed-climbing event – 'a kind of uphill slalom' – in which our companion, normally so deliberate, to his own surprise came as high as second, behind a greasy-haired barefooted young streaker in a purple nylon jockstrap.

But today, far from the smoke, sweat and financial sledgehammers, we could breathe again, in peace. We crushed cool sugary snow in our fingers and drank hot sun through half-closed eyes.

'Yes, this is a Sport. That was a Game. Fun, but just a Game.'

He handed round the pieces and beamed at us. While we chewed, he twirled his ridiculous waist-high axe, his only accessory that blissful day. He always liked to rub in the fact that he had climbed a few years nearer Raeburn than we had. 'A Wall has only two dimensions, a mountain has three; but mountaineering, you know, has *four*.' Twirl.

The Apprentice, like myself, had brought a little hammer-pick, just in case, and eyed the Doctorial weapon distastefully. 'No harm, I suppose, on a scramble like this,' he conceded, 'but bloody murder in a modern gully,' and jerked his head at one beneath us on our left. The Doctor, about to estimate – to the nearest millennium – the age of that particular geomorph, suddenly held up his hand.

'There's somebody coming up it!' We crawled and peered over.

It was not a very fierce gully. Nor modern. Just messy. Frozen mossy chock-stones, a descending gloom of aged snow and a few testy wrinkles of fairly senile ice. Its cornice, though, was of good classical architecture. We saw no one; but voices, and apparently a song, floated up from below. A grimy hole. Certainly not worth singing about.

We followed the ridge round until we could see into the gully. Yes, people were there. Four of them, roped nose-to-tail. Even at this distance we noticed the leader brandishing a long Doctorial axe. The others were gravely moving up, a step at a time. They had reached the last, icy, pitch below the cornice. They assembled there, and appeared to tie to a half-buried axe (even the Doctor was astonished – 'Damned primeval technique, no Dead Men, no ice peg!'). Then, to our complete amazement (the Doctor passed his binoculars round excitedly) one of them knelt down, another stood on his back, and a third – somehow –

clambered over them both and was raised aloft, one foot on an axe held by the second and one foot scraping on to another axe he had driven into some icy fissure. Striking up with his own axe he surmounted the crux by knees and a wriggle ('Must be tweeds', whistled the Doctor, 'otherwise he'd slide off.'), rapidly cut steps up the slope above, and crouched beneath the cornice. Another axe was passed to him by rope, he drove it in as a belay, flogged the cornice on to his companions (we heard their gusts of laughter...), then he stuck it horizontally into the now merely-vertical cornice, hauled himself up and, using it as a step and his own axe as a hook – just walked out of the gully. He lay flat on the top, recovered the second axe, tied it on, sent it down to his companions, marched well away from the edge, belayed, and brought the rest up. They emerged one by one on a tight rope some 20 feet apart.

It resembled a comic strip, a sick TV show, or an early Club photograph. 'Bloody acrobats!', declared the Apprentice, 'must have forgotten all their gear: pegs, runners, everything. What a shambles!'

But it had not looked a shambles. It had looked oddly business-like. They stood together at the top, unroping and dusting themselves. Their leader fished out a bottle and passed it round. Another pulled out a flask, and handed that round. Then – they shook hands. Shook hands.... And, mercifully, trooped away out of sight.

'Certainly,' concluded the Doctor, 'not a Modern Gully, if you can climb it that aboriginal way – 1880's, I should say.' But the climbing had appeared so simple; no primitive gropings or scrabblings. The Apprentice repeated that it had been a shambles. 'Serve 'em right if they get caught out some day, bashing on without proper equipment. Just lucky.'

Enough.... We had our own day to continue. We took in a sharp little knob to the north, above a long not very steep slope to the road, moving fast, as the weather had deteriorated. At the top, winter returned with a violent north wind, freezing us off quickly enough. Almost too quickly; for we found our descent to the road suddenly solid. It bared occasional black teeth amongst its now fish-blue iron-hard *névé*. Our vibrams were most unhappy; they shook and slithered alarmingly; would not kick steps or even scratch.

Then the blizzard hit us, driving Arctic particles about our unseen uncontrollable boots. The Apprentice and I pecked ineffectively at the slope with our baby axes; as we bent down to its gentle angle, our feet prepared to levitate. We clung. We swore. We would have to descend fifteen hundred feet sideways in socks or suchlike, it seemed, a metre a minute.

Fortunately, we had the Doctor with his despised axe. He darted about beneath us, trikes biting, and poked the pick around, winkling, slicing, carving, chopping, hacking, *willing* steps for our independently-sprung footwear. At times he fielded our feet and planted them in.

We knew we had sinned. That we should at least have brought our usual emergency line. But it was the month of May (with, alas, weather as eponymously uncertain) and a gentle slope (when we were, alas again, equipped for a steep one). So, holding each other's hand touchingly, with many a bitter oath the Apprentice and I side-stepped down, the Doctor beneath us active as some lightning conductor of the Fifth.

Of course we were bound to reach the road safely. Had not the Apprentice flashed to 5.12d? Had not he shone at Grabsworth? Were not his disengaged hand and mine clutching hammer-picks that would (if they could reach it) hook irresistibly into this next hour of glass and iron? But it would take so long. And we were so slow, and so cursed cold.

Then out of the whiteness behind us sped four figures. Skiing! No; glissading.... almost as improbably. Four tall, erect figures, their breeches and stockings unbent, their long axes – longer than the Doctor's – flicking expertly behind them.

They swung in beside us with hearty greetings. They must be the gully-climbers.

'Ha, deuced foul weather, what?' They paused, surprised, summing up our embarrassing predicament.

'I'm afraid', confessed the Doctor, gallantly sharing our blame, 'we're not really properly equipped for it....'

They looked at each other. 'No matter, no matter! We'll put you right directly!' cried the beardiest one. They all displayed white-encrusted balaclava-beards. They all looked perfectly at ease. They all wore massively-clinkered Brenva-demolishing boots.

We had little time to gape, for a rope was rapidly produced and tied – tied – round the two of us with expert knots. No jangling. We gripped it thankfully; it felt rough and hairy, stiff as a cable. We were joined to the massive anchorman behind us by a slender flexible shining one:

nylon presumably, ages old no doubt.

The Doctor turned and gazed at it with fascination as we continued jerkily down. 'Lord, it's silk... *silk*! Haven't seen one outside the Alpine Club rooooms....' He shot off downwards, having been butted by a backside-sliding Apprentice who had also, foolishly, turned to look. I followed.

With separate twangs, the Apprentice and I were arrested, amid joviality. 'Those little hammery things could be useful in some tiny gully, no doubt, but jolly old death on a big slope like this!' boomed our anchorman as he tugged us up. After that, we were lent two of their axes.

Mercifully soon, we reached the road. The sky cleared. The four, sheathed in frozen snow reinforced by a mattress of tweed, wool and whiskers, skilfully unroped us, passed round a silver-mounted hip flask, patted us paternally on the back and began to stalk off, coiling their creaking rope.

We tried to thank them and the Doctor, pointing to his car, offered a lift. Not at all, it had been Capital Fun; and their own transport lay just up the road. They vanished, with deep laughter, in which we did not join.

The Doctor shook off plaques of ice against the car and breathed on his key to thaw it. His passengers needed a strong drink for reassurance, so we drove to the nearby small hotel. We hoped to find another subject for conversation at the bar.

As soon as we stopped, one presented itself.

Bicycles. A gleaming heap by the door.

Mountain bicycles? No. 'Lord, what extraordinary contraptions!' The Doctor prodded them. Solid black monsters, with huge frames and long heads. The Apprentice, glad to shine on a day like this, polished his cycling lore and pronounced them of very old pattern – 'Late 1880's, early 1890's – and that one's just like an original Rover Safety.' We marvelled. Two of them sprouted brackets on the forks – these were fixed-wheelers, the Apprentice explained; you rested your feet there, going downhill. And look at that saddle!

We perceived that our marvellings were under scrutiny. A youngish fellow, tankard in one hand, pipe in the other. With a racing-handlebar moustache and knickerbockers of immaculate brown tweed – as were his tightly-buttoned Norfolk jacket and his cap. His ebony brogues dazzled us.

Apologies. 'Not at all. Delighted you find them of interest.' A fruity southern voice, with a firm background of stocks and shares. He quaffed, and puffed, and continued to regard us.

The Doctor hazarded: 'A cycling meet, eh?'

Puff. 'No.' Quaff.

Then, just within the door, we noticed a pile of ice axes – long, long handles and small heads. And coils of rope – hairy manila; and silk – again.

We stood and stared. Most rudely.

Our acquaintance removed his pipe and revealed a smile.

'Excuse our curiosity,' apologised the Doctor once more, indicating the axes and ropes – and boots, huge boots, far out-clinkering his own. 'but, unfortunately, you don't see many of those things today....' He then recalled that we had – indeed fortunately – seen several of those things less than an hour ago.

'Oh? I suppose it depends on who you happen to be.' A tone of amiable hauteur; and after a prolonged swig, the pipe was replaced. Still a direct gaze.

We realised what was lacking, and introduced ourselves. We shook hands. We learnt his name; familiar, but we couldn't place it. He explained that this was, in fact, a climbing meet. A meet, indeed, of the V.M.G.

V.M.G. The Doctor guessed. 'The Vintage Mountaineering Group! Excellent idea!'

'No, not quite. Almost correct, my dear fellow: but 30 years out. Not Vintage; I'd suggest that you' – he pointed his pipe-stem at the Doctor – 'you yourself are about Vintage.' He surveyed the Doctor's tweed hat, jacket, breeches, and nailed boots. 'Tricouni.... Ah, tricouni have not yet been invented, I'm glad to say. They are rather *contrived*, wouldn't you admit? Almost as much as that Eckenstein Spike. Not really Sporting – not sufficiently what you'd call in-communion-with-the-rock to be *satisfying*, don't you think?'

The pipe was replaced, alongside the smile.

('Communion with the rock,' muttered the Doctor, 'what does he want – bare feet?') However, the Apprentice, now geared to the motoring wavelength, took over from his extinguished companion. 'The Veteran Mountaineering Group!' he cried.

Our acquaintance winced a little. 'We don't in fact *approve* of that as a description,' he admitted ruefully, shaking his pipe free of emotion, 'Indeed, yesterday some of us cycled 20 miles each way to our mountain....' Certainly, he looked young and damnably fit, his hair and handle-bar glossily black. 'We prefer to be known as The Victorian Mountaineering Group.'

Just then, the gravel behind us scritched frighteningly, as four more great bicycles arrived. Their riders leapt off, swathed in ropes and rucksacks; they unwrapped long axes from the cross bars. Our rescuers, no less. Their own transport.

More people emerged from the hotel, in clouds of pipe and cigar smoke, billows of whisker and tweed, giving forth gruff and hearty welcome. With that, and further cries behind us of 'Capital, capital! My word, a fine little gully, to be sure!' it was like reading an old club journal, or an article by Campbell. Bemused, we tried to push through for our drink, now more necessary than ever.

'Ah, excuse me – the *public* bar is round at the side,' demurred our first acquaintance, directing us with his pipe. 'I fear the saloon is booked for the Group.'

Disconsolate, we were preparing to advance a hundred-odd years to the left, when one of the rescuers spotted us.

'Oh, but you must come in and celebrate our joint mountain; a first-rate Descent like that deserves something special, I do declare!'

This was a great honour. The V.M.G. were highly exclusive. Understandably so, for our torn and garish terylene and brassy zips appeared uncommonly vulgar (as they would have termed it) among the rich steamy heather- and deer-dung-textured tweediness that milled about us inside, guffawing, puffing and swallowing, shouting and singing, great feet stamping continual approbation. Only the Doctor – in a thin minor machine-stitched key – was passable, at an uneducated glance.

But our rescuers continued to bring us down safely to the Nineteenth Century. We sat at a table with them, feeling like small children who had done wrong, been forgiven, and were being allowed to stay up late with the grown-ups.

They answered our questions frankly enough. Oh they were all able to climb modern routes, if they wanted to. Some of the younger members had been international celebrities. But on their own meets, they aimed for the simple excitement of the old days, when climbing was unusual and those few who visited the hills were Gentlemen and obeyed the Rules, and dressed decently and unobtrusively. We became itchingly naked again. The Apprentice, irritated beyond endurance, unwisely pointed out that modern clothing is sooner spotted by Rescue Teams. Ah, but Rescue Teams – they smiled disarmingly – would not be needed if the Rules of the Sport were observed... (We felt too crushed to enquire if those Rules permitted three people combining tactics on an ice-pitch with one axe as belay.) No, the V.M.G. spared no effort to recapture the antique joy, they wore specially-made clothes, used specially-made equipment, rode specially-made bicycles, sported specially-grown or specially-stuck-on beards and moustaches, spoke a specially-learnt language. We thought it most tedious; Ham, in fact. But they swore that once you mastered the technique, then the enchantment and exhilaration surpassed anything you'd known on the hills before. Such Freedom, such Certainty. There was no going forward after that! Modern routes were just boring. Might as well be in a Sports Hall and do it for – money!

They met difficulties, of course. Mixing with the Contemporary Rabble eroded their own environment and provoked unseemly reactions from others. And so many things had changed for the worse. Trains no longer stopped at Highland stations, they did not accept bicycles any more, there were no Station Masters, hotels hardly ever gave decent service. Not that the V.M.G. journeyed often to North Britain, but it was the only part of Her Majesty's present dominions where they could frolic reasonably undisturbed. 'Imagine us at Harrison's or Cloggy, Langdale or Froggatt....' It had to be midweek, and out of season; today was a weekend, and see what had happened.... We drank deeper. Yes, they were mostly English, the true Romantics, but 'a few of your own club are with us, they keep it very dark of course; you'll recognise them, I'll be bound, because they won't *look* at you'; no, we had no heart to penetrate bashful and poorly-belayed beards.

North Norway was another venue. In that outback you could still do a Slingsby; but no wine, no whisky. The V.M.G. preferred the Alps, at secret vinous places with understanding inns, whence they would ascend remote and unlikely summits; the more skilful could climb right back to the 1850's, tackling peaks, passes and glaciers from goat-infested and herbicide-free *gîtes*. No, they did not use alpenstocks or ladders; nothing *silly*. And guides? Today's *führer* was most uncooperative, but porters, you could still hire porters, they were still very droll; why, only last season, old Josef...

We interrupted hastily. 'Guidebooks, anyway, are sufficient these days.' But no, they never read guidebooks, not even the latest John Ball: they *explored*. They perused little in the *Alpine Journal*, either, certainly

not after volume IX, when the rot was clearly setting in – that American, Coolidge; that dog, Tschingel; that bounder, Mummery. . . . 'But what about Harold Porter?' put in the Doctor, anxious not to appear too illiterate a Modern, 'He possessed the old spirit!' 'Precisely – and had to steam off every year to New Zealand to enjoy it. He was just greasy-poling in Europe; New Zealand in the twenties was fortunately even more backward than your Scotland.'

Fortunately, too, a gong called. 'Dinner, Gentlemen, is served.' We rose, thanked our rescuers again. Shook hands, bowed. As we sought the door, our first acquaintance reappeared, whisky and soda in grasp. He addressed the Apprentice.

'I could have sworn I'd met you before, laddie. Now I remember. You came right behind me, did you not?'

The Apprentice stared, shook his head.

Our friend glanced over his shoulder, then quickly unclipped his moustache.

'O.K.?' Grin, greasy black hair.

'It's you – Davey Baker! Of all the...'

Davey Baker, the crack speed-climb merchant in a nylon jockstrap who had beaten the Apprentice at Grabsworth by ten whole seconds two weekends ago.

The moustache replaced, David Clayton-Baker, C.A., gravely shook hands with the Apprentice, bowed to us, turned about and rejoined the other gentlemen making their way with quiet satisfaction to the Dining Room.

'Humbugs, humbugs, pretentious and doctrinaire humbugs!' exploded the Doctor, safe in the driving seat. His pride had been as much injured as ours. 'More damnably devious mock-up and make-believe in that two-faced shower than ever at Grabsworth! Just a game, a Game. Pure Egoism. No feeling for the sport at all....'

We kept hard at it, restoring our self-conceit, until the traffic and fug outside Edinburgh. Never had the three of us so agreed. They were just to be pitied, they just couldn't face Modern Life.

'Sheer bloody escapism!' pronounced the Apprentice, in conclusion. 'Pathetic. Now, where shall we go, next weekend?'

A RAVISHING WEEKEND

Well, this was D-day. We gazed across the waves. They snarled agreeably beneath our keen and thrusting prows. It was wonderful; and yet – so improbable. We were on a Seaborne Assault. A preemptive Strike. At dawn.

We were in canoes, approaching Rhum.

That weekend the Doctor and I had agreed to accompany the Apprentice to Eigg; a theoretical line up a photograph of the Sgùrr had tormented him too long. I was there to offer advice and assistance; the Doctor, to peer at fossilised pre-Tertiary landscapes and drop a top rope if necessary. We hired a motor boat from Mallaig to take us there Saturday morning, and return us too early on the Monday. The weather – necessarily – was idyllic: a long-established summer anticyclone, with no wind.

Alas, we found the Sgùrr draped with anti-idyllic Glaswegian hammerers. The Apprentice's route had long been trodden over, and even more fearsome Extremes were in screaming birth.

Sickening. We mooched over to the west coast and booted, from the singing sands of Laig, a musical feast which – meagre enough – was preferable to the one the Doctor threatened; for he had brought his pipes, and would mobilise three hundred vertical feet of basalt behind him to act as sounding board, and the whole western ocean to field his wandering grace-notes.

But Fate had intervened. We saw five splendidly fierce shark-like sea canoes drawn up on the sands, their crewmen lying alongside. Better still, the Apprentice knew one canoeist well, and the Doctor hailed another as nephew. While we prodded their beautiful beasts, they explained they had just circumnavigated Skye and were resting a couple of days – three of them in fact being unable to sit in a canoe again until Dame Nature had darned their backsides.

It was the Doctor, as usual, who inspired us. Just across the glittering sea rose the great war-peaks of Rhum – Askival, Allival, Ainshval, Barkeval, Trallval: marvellous Norwegian, Lochlanner, axe-clashing names.

We would storm them on a Viking raid. Collect all the big tops in one *fjell* swoop. We had longed to tread them, but the tiresome grovelling for permits and references had repelled us. Climbing was about Freedom, we assured ourselves. Of course, Rhum had long been attractively *Verboten*; the Doctor possessed an uncle who had lawlessly ravaged the peaks, paraded the village and bonfired the driftwood years ago in some dim Bulloughian past. But now, as a tight little island Nature Reserve, its smug monkish insularity appeared even less tolerable. Our few scruples vanished with the sun setting behind its blood-red six miles or so of defenceless water. Our fingers itched for a hilt. We would wrest the summits from those sanctimonious clerics, send them fleeing with their precious apparatus and manuscripts; we would bring Battle, Fire and Rapine. The pomp and panoply of State-Supported Science offered rich booty to Pirate Enterprise, more satisfying than the nineteenth-century leavings of some Lancashire cotton-bobbiner. It would be Nae Bother At Aa. Sure Thing. Thor would Rule O.K.

We were well qualified for Assault. The Apprentice had slalomed canoelets through Tay, Spey and Findhorn. I had paddled among detergents in the Firth of Froth. The Doctor, reputedly an expert with the Canadian variety, had (he said) descended the Mackenzie, even been in one of Vaillancourt's birch-barks; and, more relevantly, claimed to have out-kayaked a triple-rolling Sir Hector Macassar off Angmagssalik. No problem there.

Fortunately, the owners were equally enthusiastic. The two who could still turn another cheek to the job would accompany us as off-shore escorts – for safety. (Safety! On a Viking Raid...) We would start at dawn, be back victorious by evening.

We practised each in his own canoe, learning about tetchety rudders, about wave-slicing, and how to keep on continuous terms with 17-odd feet of mind-of-its-own thoroughbred. Hunters they were, not hacks; killer whales, to vary the necessary macho metaphor.

So here we were, then, the following morning, approaching Rhum. Cold, wet, with raw backsides; but our deadly dragon-headed galleys snaked purposefully, mercilessly, in. We avoided the bays of Papadil and Dibidil and chose a less conspicuous and more appropriate sandy inlet by the cliffs at Rudha nam Meirleach, Cape of the Thieves. Our escort tactfully dropped back, to paddle about a bit and meet us here later.

Our keels grated in an authentically sinister fashion. We sprang ashore, the Doctor catching his paddle between his legs and executing a vigorous and oath-splashing somersault, a display of virtuosity which terrified the natives, for not one was to be seen. We dragged our steeds up the turf and lashed them to old driftwood, in case of a great wave being engendered by the curse of some bathymetrically-minded cleric; and hid the paddles among the many boulders nearby.

We raced across welcome grass to Beinn an Stac, as exhilarated after our voyage as Leif Ericsson himself. Then up and along the wonderful spear-brandishing ridge from Askival to Ainshval, its gendarme falling swiftly to our arms. Below us, a super-Aegean blue of sea, and the emerald aircraft-carrier of Eigg. And right beneath our feet – the proper place – Kinloch Castle and all its accoutrements, clearly in a state of panic.

We roared and stamped and projected runic V-signs in victory, but did not work ourselves up – or down – sufficiently to descend in fury upon the prostrate inhabitants. We really had not time to go berserk if we were to get back to Eigg that night for the motorboat next morning. Still, we managed to bear off the nine prize peaks of the ridge, and ravished a few of the better-looking pitches on Ruinsival. No one else to be seen. The island had been ours. Our only near casualty was the Doctor's Low G finger, just missed by a stone from above, which the Apprentice denied came from him but was an Act of Odin – besides, bagpipes were instruments unworthy of a Viking; and anyway, why should the Doctor complain, what was a finger or two to a piper like himself?

Battle, Fire and Rapine – all except the Fire for, despite the beckoning accumulation of driftwood in the western cliffs, our only matches had been in the Doctor's back breeches pocket and he had sat for too long in too much water on the way across.

Regretfully law-abiding to that extent, we bounded down from above Papadil in the lengthening light. And then right in our path we saw a group of people gathered on the cliff edge, peering over. Around them lay instruments of various sorts and they were jabbering together angrily. Obviously monks. There were too many of them to kill effectively at the end of a tiring day; and, having pushed attack and foray so successfully all those hours, we did not welcome the indignity of being seized as trespassers. We would, Vikings though we indubitably were, prefer any confrontation to be delayed until we got between them and our – now agonizingly naked – vessels beneath.

We wrapped our rope in an anorak and skipped round behind them, bog to bog, until well below.

Then the Apprentice fell over a stone, and it echoed along the cliffs. Sixteen eyes swivelled upon us. More furious jabbering; shouts; and they plunged down.

They met us at the boats. They carried sticks and telescopic metal rods. They shook with emotion.

While they were getting their breath back, the Doctor seized his opportunity.

'Can we help you?' he enquired, sweetly. 'You seemed worried about something up there....'

They nodded. Their leader, no doubt some Abbot or other, broke out: 'You could be most useful.'

'We thought we might be,' flashed in our crafty companion, 'We were just off-shore.'

Outraged ghosts of Thorfinn Bloody-Fist, Magnus Bareleg, Harald War-Tooth, Ivar-of-the-Long-Reach, disowned us, turned away. Bargaining with, creeping before, vermin like that. Next thing, we should all be Converted. Christened B.Sc. or something.

'Have you, by any chance, a *rope*?' the worthy one enquired, clasping his hands together in appeal.

We sniffed a trap, to lure us into Confession. We fingered swords belligerently. The ghosts looked back, and brightened. But the Doctor cut in.

'We have our sea-line, if that'd be any use – we thought it might, you know, that's why we brought it ashore....' True; and he undid the camouflage.

Relief on both sides. Amicable chatter. It seemed there was a nest of the white-tailed eagle (*Halliaeetus albicilla*, no less) on these cliffs, not far indeed from Sròn na h-Iolaire, Eagle Point; one of Rhum's very own brood, the second generation of Norwegian colonists invited here by these same clerics we had just refrained from massacring. Two nests, in fact, side by side, extremely precious – the Abbot rolled up his eyes – but both at this minute endangered by a huge teetering lump of turf dislodged by some lay-brother in their party who had been erecting a tripod.

The Abbot implored us to lend him the rope and to tie a good sailor's knot in it so that he could be lowered to the impending turf. He was no climber but... his faith demanded any sacrifice.

We all of course jumped in: O but we were not much of climbers either but we did understand knots and ropes – seafarers, voyagers on great waters, needed to.

All this resulted in the Apprentice leading a quite fine upward traverse and, at its end, kicking the offending clod into the sea, just starboard of our returning escort. A pendulum back, and an abseil down.

Uplifted hands from the brethren (and a sister). Blessings and apologies showered upon us; although one (maybe the laybrother) had regarded the Apprentice's climbing skill with an unpleasingly knowing smile.

'They are so valuable, the little eaglets,' sighed the Abbot. 'We have suffered raiders here, too, you know.' We shifted uncomfortably, avoiding the laybrother's (squint) eye. 'Raiders, egg-thieves, who came by powerboat and ransacked our only three nests last spring.... So selfish – years of devoted work gone for nothing' – and he dropped his hands piteously.

'Shocking, shocking,' murmured our chief Viking, 'no decency whatever; can't understand it.' 'Vandals,' put in the Apprentice, still reeking of recent gore, 'bloody vandals.' 'Mean sods, do anything for loot,' we agreed.

Beside us, our longships turned on their keels in disgust, they began to slither back to the rising tide, would no longer bear such cowards, lily-lips, turncoats. We grabbed their prows; the dragons' heads had already vanished.

Worse was to come. We were invited back in Land Rovers to the Castle Canteen. And to a slide show on the Smaller Mammals of South East Asia.

We came to our senses. This was no right end to a Viking Raid. We demurred.

'O but of course you can stay at the Castle. We could take you over to Eigg, canoes and all, in the morning.' Etc., etc.

'Are you quite sure?' We were quite sure.

Handshakes – handshakes! – all round. We sauntered down as insolently heroic as we could, ground the pebbles beneath our heels, and strapped on a bravado of golden lifejackets. Then we began to launch our steeds: and remembered about the damned paddles. The Apprentice and I dashed back among the boulders where we had hidden them – but there were dozens of boulders.... The Doctor, struggling with three very restive half-floating charges – which had entangled their leads and now jumped up and down like excitable and enormously elongated Afghan hounds - shouted useless advice and splashed unhappily. All of which detracted from our former magnificence of departure. With curses and bruised knees the Apprentice and I leapt from slimy rock to slimy rock. The clerics looked on, bewildered. Then that unpleasantly-grinning laybrother detached himself, ambled to a further group of boulders, and reappeared with our paddles. They were behind a stone, he said. We thanked him (he should have been the first one slaughtered).

When we had unwound the various leads from each other, we stepped into our craft – which felt decidedly cool towards us – and thrust out over the winking Atlantic. We heard grateful prayers behind us, but never looked back. We warmed once more to self-respect and forged through the blood-boltered sun-setting surf towards our piratical lair, boasting to admiring escorts of the violent deeds done. We would feast that night to wild music, on sausages roasted black by a flaming primus, and drain whisky and McEwan's from polished skulls.

Which we more or less did. We lay – we avoided sitting – beside a blaze of driftwood after our feast, and swore that henceforth we should wield axe and pick with renewed vigour, hammer without mercy; that Haston was right, that there was nothing like freedom, absolute freedom from bourgeois values, to bring out the best in climbing.

Next spring we would be back for eggs.

DROPPING IN

A classical early spring day. Blue sky, marble snow. And a classical early route – Y-Gully of Cruach Ardrain. The Apprentice, cured of boils on the backside (a relic of last year's Rhum trip) by a potently patent prescription of the Doctor's, agreed that the least we could do was to join our nostalgic friend on such a comfortably old-fashioned and uneventful climb; anyway, he preferred not to risk his newly-repaired upholstery just yet by any abrasive high-Grade contortions. A nice walk like this would do fine.

So we had ambled up in crampons, drinking in the clear air, and the Doctor had skipped along behind – not all that far behind – with axe and tricounis, whistling execrably. He was strapped into a huge rucksack – which carried skis – so his performance was the more commendable. But we had to rope him when it got steep.

Why the huge rucksack? Mystery. Why skis? Mystery... he surely did not intend to ski down Y-Gully! Not enough snow elsewhere. In Kandahar bindings – and he had brought no sticks.... Mystery, also, why our companion kept stopping – on bulges of verglas we carefully avoided – apparently to sniff the air and study the few (but increasing) white clouds that sailed above. Taking omens, we judged. Up to something.

The cornice was a large Edwardian mantelpiece, safe as in houses. We hauled up the damned skis, their purpose still darkly unexplained; if he wanted to ski the gully, we would just tie him up.

At the cairn the Apprentice and I dismissed the thought, and prepared for the usual Doctorial summit lounge. But no, he was hopping about, still sniffing, wetting his forefinger and holding it up; and casting paper from our jammy pieces into the air. We gently remonstrated, puzzled. And turned our attention to the great white distances of Black Mount, the vast sweep of Beinn Dòrain, and the piebald heads of Glencoe, Nevis and the Mamores above the haze.

Much rustling behind. We looked over our shoulders.

Heavens, what was this? He had disembowelled his rucksack and was shaking out an enormous multicoloured sleeping-bag affair, with strings like spiders' legs – a parachute-harness sort of thing.

'Could you chaps stand and hold me down – on these ropes here – while I strap it tight? Got to be jolly careful to do the right thing, you know – can't abseil off an up-current....'

We paled. No, it was not a collapsible hang-glider. Nor a parachute for that Extreme Ski descent of Y-Gully. But a little of both, in fact: the Doctor was preparing to Paraglide....

We had watched practitioners of this hybrid craft the previous summer; and concluded that – as rain could collapse the para part – any gliding with such an assemblage in the Scottish hills would be rapidly down the vertical component. As for wearing skis as well.... Easy enough on Everest; but here....

The Doctor had secretly practised on expensive evenings through the unusually dry autumn. And now modestly claimed he would, 'Just nip off the top here, and see you down in the glen there – as near as the end of the snow and the start of the trees as possible. Of course, I could land sooner if I wanted to – just pull on these strings and close the tubes. But I'd like to make a record of it – the wind's dead right.' And, as he strapped and buckled and patted his harness ('doesn't come undone easily, I can tell you; this is a new type, won't let you out in a hurry – absolutely safe!'), he threw at us observations on thrusts, thermals, downdraughts, updraughts... and the rest of the airy fancies of his vaporous trade.

'The very thing for a *quick* descent. Better than simply skis, you don't need snow, you're quite independent of terrain. So restful. You just sit up there; all too briefly, I'm afraid. Marvellous if you could dangle for hours above a distant earth....' He prattled on.

It sounded convincing enough, but the immense vacuum in front of us and below did not appear to bear the weight of enquiry. We drew back.

'You chaps carry my sack and axe and things for me, will you? I'll wait for you down there, or walk up and meet you; don't be too long.'

He shuffled into his long Neanderthal skis. We two looked at each other.

The Doctor gathered the various strands we had been anchoring. 'Now, keep out of my way. I'll start from the cairn.'

We watched his improbable figure, ballooning in crinoline skirt and

Bedouin cloak, as it billowed about the cairn. Then, engines roaring, it turned into the slipstream from the cornice and began to slide towards the edge.

Unfortunately, some string or other caught on a boulder, and progress was dramatically halted.

Unravelled again, and oblivious of our by-now almost frantic pleas for him to give it up, be sensible, think of the rocks, think of the ice, he taxied rapidly past us once more.

As the air, miraculously, puffed into his counterpaning robes, his skating strides grew longer and more dreamlike; so that at the last of the Apprentice's admonitions – appropriately enough 'For Heaven's sake, come off it!' – he toed delicately from the cornice, fluttered alarmingly, and disappeared, like an inflatable double bed, into the abyss.

Then he reappeared to our aghast eyes, bumpiting upwards on a surge, spinning wildly like a long-legged frog in his harness. We ran to the edge. He was floating down again, perilously near the rock, his canopy plucking out loose stones, showers of them; then the hickory kicked a crag and he pushed off at last, alarmingly detached from Scotland.

Happily airborne. The fresh wind, now clearly north, caught him and he soared away, legs flailing like an excited heron, away into a wavering kaleidoscopic dot growing fainter and fainter. He went a hell of a distance, bundled along like litter. It seemed, too, as if one ski had come loose, dangling by a safety-strap.

A passing cloud engulfed us; the weather was deteriorating. When it cleared, he was out of sight. Well, he had passed airborne over the roughest part; and appeared to be safely delivered between Grey Heights and Stob Coire Bhuidhe, towards the snowy grass and green forests below. He might even have broken his record; though skis, legs or neck seemed likelier casualties.

The Apprentice and I picked up the luggage and jerked away down, almost in envy. We enjoyed a good stiff glissade, thigh-burning and tooth-loosening. Then, galumphing down slushy rushes and heather, we scanned the upcoming hectares for him or his heliotropic marquee – which should have been visible for miles, however tattered.

No sign. He must have landed, packed up, and walked down the

forestry tracks. We marched about them, hallooing. No answer. It was growing dark. We dropped to the car; nothing. To the hostel: nobody had seen a... parachutist – one with skis.... They stared at us strangely. We combed the rides again, shouting and cursing. Some hostellers, intrigued, joined us.

Darkness proved a blessing. We heard a cry and raced to it; it was a hosteller who had seen a light, up in the sky, moving. Not a star, not a comet – he studied astronomy, he knew. *There*. It glittered above a few vigorous hectares of 50-foot Sitka spruce. Was it the Doctor? Lord, was he *still* gliding?

We pushed closer. It was clearly waving; high up; far in the wood. Near the point of a leading shoot – or a leading ski. Stationary; he was anchored to something.

We sent down for billhooks, axes, long poles. All kinds of medieval Bannockburnian instruments trooped up; Crianlarich was agog. Plus a couple of incredulous forestry workers, power-sawed for snedding branches. We set to work – after filling in a form with name, rank and number of the astronaut, in case of injury to Commission employees.

He was amongst the upper whorls of a very aggressively-unshaven *Picea sitchensis*. He appeared inextricably entangled, skis, ski-bindings, great primary branches and infinite needles embracing his integument. It took two hours – and much of the tree – to get him down. By now a large torch-wielding crowd had assembled, and the lop-and-top was speedily cleared. The bird-watchers were particularly interested, all binoculars raised; but not a nest could be seen.

Considering he had achieved both his desires – a quick descent, and dangling for hours above a distant earth – the Doctor seemed subdued as he climbed stiffly down the last few branch-stubs, still in harness. The Apprentice had gathered up most of the arboreal knitting, and roped down through the flicker of torch-beams engulfed in it like a drifting jelly-fish, a midnight *Medusa*. The skis had been pushed down earlier, scraping through the Velcro of a million needles. Apparently the one dangling board had caught in the tree on the way over – 'Just as I was going so well, could easily have made the main road,' the Doctor had informed us from his eyrie, above the smoke and roar of power-saws.

Most of the delay stemmed from our companion's tiresome insistence on preserving as much of the costly integrity of his fabric as possible. Moreover, his extra-specially-secure buckles had jammed immovably shut with bits of twig and sliced needle; and the Doctor firmly opposed prising them open or cutting harness or cords – 'We rely absolutely on these things!' Wrapping his committee-sized toga about him, he strode off along the aisles of the forest through a cheering gallery of torches, like a wounded archangel, his trailing wings carried behind him by eager acolytes. The Apprentice, bearing aloft crossed skis, solemnly completed this hierarchical procession.

Disdaining emotional invitations to the hostel, where local theatricals were to be performed that night, we made for the car, after thanking our bushwackers and gilding the much-soured foresters. The Doctor was as embarrassed as we have seen him. He had particular reason that weekend to avoid Publicity. A colleague of his had, a few days earlier, been celebrated in the press and ridiculed by his profession for unseemly exhibitionist conduct – 'Daredevil Medical Flies Own Helicopter to Snowed-In Patient'; apparently all the patient had needed was a packet of paracetamol, and his doctor a set of winter tyres. Our companion was unusually scathing; we suspected he had himself been reminded about some of our own unhappily-reported misadventures in the past.

Anyway, he refused to drive, cocooned as he was, even if we draped his chrysalis over the seat behind him. 'Suppose some fool skidded into us – the roads are hellish slippery tonight.... bound to get in the papers.' He crawled into the back to pupate, until we had driven him to a fellow-enthusiast at Killin who had experience and tools for the job. I was picked to drive, for the north wind had brought quite a blizzard, and the Apprentice disliked the huge old Merc, even on good roads.

I disliked it on these roads. Despite hoarse encouragement from the shrouds behind, I manoeuvred its dour slithering Teutonicity with uneasy tenderness.

A few miles further, lights waved, and we slid to a halt. Accident. The Doctor groaned. We two clambered out. Apparently an ambulance coming up had met a skiing-bus going down, and both now reclined across the road, heads irretrievably in the ditch. No casualties fortunately, except the two ambulance men – shocked – and a doctor in his car following the ambulance, who biffed it heartily; and had already been despatched southwards dazed, nursing a broken arm, followed by the equally bemused ambulance men.

So... the road would be blocked a long long time. The Doctor was well wrapped up, but we all suffered hunger and rage. Curse, curse. Then, an anguished head appeared at the window. 'Nobody here a doctor?' It seemed very worried. 'Kitty's in bad trouble....' We recalled a previous discomfiture with a damned cat, and were about to explode with a further oath, when the unwilling and mummified Hippocrates in the back hushed us and asked for details.

Harrowing ones. Kitty, who lived in a cottage on the big estate opposite, was having trouble delivering her fourth bairn two weeks early. I shall spare the details, but clearly the half-asphyxiated semi-infant had to be freed; the local wise women could not disentangle it, and the phoned-for Rescue Party – doctor and ambulance – had been effectively wiped out by the Denny, Dennyloanheid and Dunipace Cooperative Wholesale Society Rambling and Ski Club bus on its way to an evening ceilidh at Killin. Speed was vital.

I wearily urged the bucketing beast up the track to the cottage. We stuck halfway, and the Doctor – good soul – staggered out in his acreage of nighties into the blast; then – O most excellent soul and to the wonder of the milling crowd of locals (it was a flourishing estate, for once) – he flashed out a knife and cut his own cords....

The – I suppose – afterbirth billowed into the throng, whose smaller fry seized it joyfully. 'Look after it, now! I need it again!' – and we three trudged to the cottage.

No need to describe further. Our companion is proficient at obstetrics (as he needs to be, with his kind of mountain tent) and soon had the little stranger out of his predicament and into the steaming basin-slopping back bedroom. A loud howl announced success to us outside the door. Fine boy. We two were then regaled most alcoholically by delirious father, uncles and other thirsty next-of-kin; while the Doctor dilated within to assembled amateur midwives. Mr Bruce was so hospitable that the Apprentice soon could scarcely converse coherently, certainly not stand.

So that when the inevitable happened an hour or so later – after a splendid meal cooked by multiple aunts – and a pack of police and journalists flooded in, the Apprentice was seized for interview: the Doctor, horrified, had locked himself up, and I was being harangued by some hugely protective neighbour – 'Jist you be keeping yerself awaay from those kind o fellies, now... they're aall lies!'

The reporters had met crowds of sprogs parading about under the moon (all snow had ceased) with a Parachute. It was the one the New Doctor had come in! He was going to use it again! He always came in it! The journalists had photographed the held-up contraption from all angles, and now desired words from the intrepid aviator. They were baying with delight.

Even they could not mistake the boozed Apprentice for our worthy companion, but – hungry for bread – they took, alas, their Story from his grievously disconnected discourse.

Under such circumstances it is possibly understandable, almost excusable, if Kitty Bruce becomes confused with Sitka spruce. And that the graphic description of our friend's inextricable landing from 2000 feet on top of the latter, grows irresolvably entangled with his dramatic release of the former.

So much so, that – while the less mendacious newspapers next day carried the story of how gallant Doctor ____ (full name) had parachuted down through a blizzard to deliver a baby – their more imaginative fellows described how Dr ____ had not only parachuted down to deliver a baby (a feat he performed throughout the Highland winter) but had delivered it at the top of a 50-foot conifer.

And how did his name get out? Ask, maybe, the forestry workers, who had howked and hacked about him long enough: for – maybe again – insufficient reward.

Anyway, he has not yet been back to measure his long-distance Record. The other one scaled 8½lbs.

A KINDRED CLUB

We hadn't climbed together for some time. The Apprentice had taken to collecting ('knocking off' was his injudicious term) frozen waterfalls; I, preferring ice cooked a little longer, joined some friends to gather as many Nevis gullies as we could in 24 hours; the Doctor – on his only patient-free weekend – streaked across a dissolving last stage of the *Haute Route Ecossaise* (version No. 6) between one thaw and the next, completing at last that very fluid itinerary. So we all felt sufficiently well-fed and self-satisfied to enjoy together a simple unclimbed Grade II up one of the few subsidiary Tops still unbitten by Doctorial tricounis. A final snack, a mere Munro mint, after those more demanding statistical orgies.

On the way down we passed a loch, frozen and snow-covered.

'Good Lord, there's a tent on it.' So there was. 'Damned fools. I suppose they *know* it's a loch....'

We went over. The Doctor shook his head. 'They'd get a shock if a thaw came. Or a Water-Horse.' (It was the winter after our West Highland haunting, and he was still somewhat sensitive to the paranormal).

The flaps were open. We looked in. Heavens!

There was a great hole in the floor. Flakes of ice lay round it; and, in it, black water licked thirstily.

The evidence was horrifyingly clear: a sleeping bag crumpled beside it, a primus that cooked the last meal beyond it, a rucksack spilled in the corner; and an ice axe, glazed with ice, overhanging the edge.

'Fallen through! He'd tried to climb out with the axe, but just broke off more of the edge. Soon chilled in this water....'

Dreadful. Nothing we could do now. The Apprentice poked his axe down; but met only welcoming gurgles. We straightened, and looked about helplessly. There were footprints all round: presumably his companions – we had noticed tents further down the hill – had tried to assist. Maybe they had pulled him out, here or elsewhere.

Then we saw a figure approaching through the dusk. 'One of the rescue team!' His walkie-talkie aerial bobbed importantly as he plowtered across.

He was a cheery cove, considering. His red face beamed from an eiderdown of jackets. Perhaps they *had* been successful.

'Any luck?' the Doctor asked him, suitably serious.

'Nane at aa. I've been round the shore, breakin it up' – here he brandished a kind of alpenstock – 'not a sign. So I'll just awa into the tent and drum up; and wait. There's always hope. There's always tonight and tomorrow.'

We gaped. The Doctor was shocked. 'He'd need to be a *fish* for you to get him out alive by then,' he exclaimed severely, but humouring the fellow's levity.

'He would so. Or back he goes in!'

This was too much, even for Survival Euphoria. The Doctor, biting his lip – after all it was his trade, or would have been had we got there earlier – asked if others beside our rather too equable acquaintance were on the lookout: 'for a bite,' he added, as further reproof.

'Aye, there's Andy down at the big loch, and Chairlie on the wee lochan up top. Nae luck yet, any o 'em.'

We swayed. Three people looking for three different campers fallen through three different lochs. No....

Then we saw the aerial was a fishing rod.

Things became clearer, though scarcely more probable.

Inside the tent, carefully round the hole, down which our friend – Boab – had now slipped his line for the night, we snuggled together, drank scalding tea laced with some breath-stopping rum-like liquor, and were regaled with the story of the S.M.A.C. – the The Scottish Mountain Angling Club.

Its members fished lochs – only lochs, mind, rivers and burns were a different thing altogether – lochs, as high as they could. The higher, the better. For the higher the loch, the more difficult it became: less fish, and more crafty – 'No so easy taken in.' But they had to be fish. Other things, you threw back.

They possessed a list – Topwater's Tables, they called them, after some probably legendary map-scouring old member – of all the separate mountain lochs over 1000 feet in Scotland; and a subsidiary list of the wee lochans ('aye, an some o *them*'s the best'). The joy lay not only in catching your fish – trout, char, eel or whatever – but in ticking off the lochs, the Topwaters, you caught them in. *That* made it really popular –

'gave you something to bite on.' The experts could go very high, with special equipment; alloy gaffs and landing nets, high altitude lines and baits – high-flies in fact: not the low-country Hecham Pechams, not the Black and Blae, but the latest Goretex ones, Neviscast, K2-Killer, Mustagh Toorie, Messner's Indispensable, Bonington's Glory, McInnes' Raised Hackle.... Some people would try anything to catch higher.

For it wasn't the weight or the length of the fish that counted for the S.M.A.C. – it was the height. And very few exceeded 2500 feet, Boab told us. But Andy, Andy had catched a fine little 3721-footer that very summer in Lochan Buidhe above Loch Avon. They measured in feet because feet seemed higher than metres – the idea of 'Bathymetros' was nonsense. Or fathoms – fathoms went down, not up. Feet was the logical thing. It was great, collecting Topwaters. They had another list, of who had done what lochs. They were starting furth of Scotland, too.

There seemed no end to this piscatorial puerility.

'But surely,' argued the Doctor, aware of Sin, 'surely you'll get some characters taking up fish specially to stock a high loch previously uncli-, uncaught-in?'

'Ah, that's Artificials. That's no fair. You've to fish free, or with a proper aid. Anyway, if you cheat once, you never feel the same again. All the fun's out of it.' No, that's why they never had false entries. Every loch they had caught a fish in, they had caught a fish in. If you couldna – that was Sport, eh? You might be lucky next time; or you might really have reached the altitudinal limit.

What was the limit? No one knew. That's what made it hook you, so to speak. It depended, too, how far east or west you were – climatic, like with plants. Every month, every week, someone would report a new loch they'd caught a fish in, a First Landing. They dug a wee puddle beside it, to let others know. So the Tables grew and grew, and the altitudes were pushed higher and higher....

We felt envious. The Golden Age. Robertson, Munro, Phillip and Corner, Gall Inglis, all over again. Everests piled upon Everests, on our doorstep. And what about Winter Fishing?

'A-ha-ha, yon's the thing, now. More skill, more challenge. Fish dinna want to feed in winter. You have to make 'em interested, really hungry, like.' There existed a whole range of Winter Mountain Angling techniques and tackle. Casting by compass in a whiteout; ice-screws for making a hole. And bait: only the top men used Ice Flies, the rest dangled flexible kernmantel worms; or a contraption called a Mountain-Fisherman's Friend – an alloy device whose glitter attracted window-shopping fish and, when they came close enough, snapped two metal jaws across them – 'Clap! Just like that!' Friends were expensive: bottoms of lochs were scoured for other people's lost Friends, and Friends tended to go missing at Meets, even at those of so respectable a club as the S.M.A.C.

The Doctor, though no great fisherman ('Look what happened to Collie!'), had fished through holes in ice abroad. Boab shook his head. 'Aye, but Scottish Winter Mountain Angling is a thing on its own, ken. The ice here is *different*. Humidity, the Gulf Stream. And the fish is more intelligent. People come from all over the world to fish these mountain lochs, lads.'

Of course they had a Club Song, Guidebooks, Annual Dinners, Journal.... We became increasingly uncomfortable. Did they have women members? asked the Apprentice sourly. 'Ah, yon's a great question with some kind o folk. Ye see, there *is* a women's club – the Scottish Ladies' Mountain Fishing Association of Edinburgh, Aberdeen and Glasgow: but that's too bloody exclusive, ken – what about aa those fra Dundee, Stirling, Ayr, Kirrie, Inverness, Dalbeattie and suchlike places? Eh?'

It seemed Boab might not rise to the direct question. The Doctor therefore cast, to windward, a more carefully-tied remark: 'So, quite a few women fish Topwaters?' 'Och, women catch fish as well as men, man. But, masel, I wouldna go as far as thae Mixed Rods, sharin the same bait, like. An there's an awfy lot o blether, wi wifies up an down your loch; nae Serious Talk. Mind you, they tie the flies no bad. The young lads likes the idea, nae wonder, but na, na, no for me.' He spat into the hole. After a reassuring swig, he continued more confidently into Bairns' Clubs (the 'High Fry' led there, it seemed) and decried the increasing number of mountain fishers ('the banks is trampled awa, lochs is fillin up'), commercialism and competition tactics everywhere. More spits. We rose to go.

Boab pressed toffee upon us. 'And what are you lads doing here anyway? Climbing, eh? Just gaun up to come down? Seems a daft-like kind o a ploy – beggin yer pardon, o course. Nae time for Reflection. An awfy *waste* o a day.' We feebly inferred the delights and heroics, the Spiritual Fulfilment, of winter cliffs, gullies, ridges, slabs. Scenery, and that.

'But ye dinna get *fish* out o them? There's nae *Rationality* behind it? Canna see the sense, masel. But let everybiddy tak his ain line – that's the Club Motto.'

Here Boab's particular one registered communication with Beneath. We backed out, avoiding the edge, so he could conquer undistracted.

'Aye, aye, boys, cheero. Look in on Andy on the way down. He'll tell you some fine tales, some gey queer-like gauns-on in these lochs. Ach, ye____ ! Ye___ !'

He had not ticked off that loch, at any rate.

We did not look in on Andy on the way down. The Doctor several times began to question the existence of such people. 'Imagine grown men (and women!) behaving like that! Going through all those complications of discomfort and – let's face it – danger for the sake of a wretched ego-trip! Dreaming up fake ethics, grotesque regulations, to excuse it! Among this magnificent landscape.... What a waste of good mountains! Why....' He checked himself repeatedly. He found he could say very little.

In fact, none of us could say very much. Beinn Fhada looked down sympathetically.

'I'll get a copy of the Club Song, anyway,' he remarked at the car. 'We'll sing it at the next Dinner. Should go down well, after the Soup.'

THE RISKS OF EXPOSURE

The Doctor brings tiresome habits to the hill. Photography, for example. Recently, attacks of the click have become more pernicious, because less predictable. Before, symptoms were obvious; we could avoid him. His outline swelled, he swayed as in advanced pregnancy. We fled. The unperceptive were caught, forced to nurse a litter of satchels – 'So I can keep my hands free for a quick shot....'; to dandle them for hours while he delivered himself of various lenses; or to descend wearily on some Mercy Mission for the odd dropped adaptor – 'It's a small ring, silvery, you'll easily see it in the heather; about half a mile back....'

Zooms have changed all that. Even two zooms – an infinity of lenses – can lurk in a small rucksack. The mania incubates unseen. Especially as the Doctor no longer carries a tripod. His collapsible Litewate Tripod, a detestable appendage contrived by some surrealist Manxman, collapsed expensively a year or so back. He used it for a delayed action picture of an Easter Meet. The first time, he set the camera off before he rushed over to join us; the next time, he rushed over to join us but forgot to let go of the cable release; the third time, he let go of the cable release and rushed over and joined us but the thing got spasms and took a photograph backwards. The fourth time it stared straight at us and didn't go off at all, and the Doctor marched back to reset it and got a blast of Ektachrome bang in the stomach. In those days we could watch, and keep away. Zooms are hidden and treacherous. They can be pulled on you like a gun.

Because of this, we were badly caught last summer. We went to Ardgour, to do something on Garbh Bheinn next day. In the tent the Doctor sprung on us a Great Photographic Competition, sponsored, appropriately enough, by the then Highlands and Islands Development Board. Prizes were in four categories: The Beauties of Nature; Landscape; Action; and Humorous (Funnies). The Doctor was determined to enter all four, and zoomed and unzoomed beside the roaring primus.

'This lens is damned good: 35 to 105, macro setting, splendid resolution, no flare, no distortion.... Should do the whole lot tomorrow no bother; just bought a new film. We'll start with the Beauties of Nature!'

Zoom. Zoom.

We groaned. But the Apprentice fingered his Compact – usually reserved for his second's disasters. 'Might try an action shot....' he mused above blue smoke and ebony sausages.

Next day's good weather therefore had drawbacks. We were first delayed by prolonged breathing on, and polishing of, the zoom. Then the Doctor had to blow and brush out his Canon's body cavity with surgical deliberation before inserting the new film. He was thrilled by a long golden hair he extracted. 'How *could* it have got in? And where from?' Impatiently we attributed it to some previous Beauty of Nature and ushered him, still trichophilic, on to the hill. It may well have been his wife's, when she was younger.

Once there, we buckled down to Nature. Nature was doing a big thing that morning. It hummed, whistled, bloomed and seeded no end. We pointed out to the Doctor pretty blossoms and jolly tweets. We were doubtless irritating. But the real dig for button-smackers is always Carnivorous Plants, and the Doctor ensconced himself appreciatively beside a Greater Sundew, screwing its gullet into focus. This talented vegetable had recently taken on board a fairly fat bluebottle which was now, alas, a mere eviscerated hulk. It raised a salivating gob hopefully towards its admirer. Begging for more.

And just then another large buzz of bluebottle did plop into his sundew and began, with inaudible bellowings, to become enmeshed. The Doctor, swithering too long between Beauties of Nature and Common Humanity, could only retrieve an irremediably digested *Callimorpha vomitoria*. Sentimental about flowers, he returned the plateful to its indignant owner. Not much there. What next?

We led him to various pleasing possibilities. A monumentally wide-spreading cowpat was carefully inspected, the Doctor insisting that such places held a large and varied population; the Apprentice assured him Glasgow Was Miles Better. After an exceptionally-dead sheep and several sardonic birds, the Doctor finally fell for a parasitic Lousewort which, despite name and habits, glowed pink in the sun. Several shots at that. Good.

Over to landscape. It filled the rest of the morning. If the Great Glen Fault had ambled a mile further on, the Doctor could have netted a superb perspective of Bidean; as it was, Sgòrr Dhònuill got in the way.

Lochaber remaining unmoved, we had to shift more amenable *décor*. Under direction, the Apprentice and I tore away interfering branches of native trees with a zeal worthy of the Forestry Commission. This done, the Apprentice was dismissed twenty-five yards down to Pose; he gazed sympathetically towards the site of execution of James Stewart of Appin.

'No; a little to the left – STAY *THERE* – *look* a little to the left; head up, chin in, don't scratch your backside – all right, scratch it once; *once*, dammit. Fine...!'

But the artist was not yet satisfied. ('Hmmm....') The Human Interest had to remove his own shirt ('Hopeless colour – doesn't go at all!') and put on mine; and re-enter his (now much trampled) Foreground. ('Hmm, aah; hmm.') I had to stand on the right and drape a careless spray of birch before the lens. 'Hmm, hmm – *and* on the left.' This was clearly impossible unless the Apprentice came up to help; when he would no longer be down there. So I drove in a piece of long-suffering willow on the left and held out my offering on the right.

'Splendid!' cried the Doctor, about to press. Whereupon the Apprentice, hearing and unhappily anticipating, turned with relief and climbed back towards us. He had to be driven down again and be fitted once more, minutely and with abuse, into the landscape.

Ready? But then People began to arrive, plugging inexorably across the field of view. First a cheery and apparently deaf couple collecting Corbetts. Then a man gathering beetles. Then some fellow with a ginger dog who desired the Doctor's opinion on The Depopulation of the Highlands. Then a lady needing a Ranger. Then a shepherd with a gun looking for some bloody fool with a ginger dog. Then the beetle man coming down. Through them all, the Apprentice stared stonily eastward; Appin and Lochaber, arms about each other's neck, beamed back. The Doctor grew pale and drawn.

Then who should appear but Geordie and Wull, on the same misguided mission as ourselves, Geordie lugging his great mahogany and brass contraption and trailing a tripod limbed with steel, Wull festooned with the expensive consequences of his usual duplicatory precautions – though having only two jobs he failed to extend to a hexapod.

We were not overpleased to see them thus arrayed. Twice before we had suffered from their photographic deliberations. Once during our

Freeze-in on The Dreepie, and more recently at Gunpowder Green when the Doctor, entering backwards in his socks, had overturned the primus and set the tent alight. That was a bad affair. We had escaped with most things except some hair, a dozen eggs and the tent, but as we raked the smouldering debris, weeping and cursing, the Apprentice frantic for his new Goretex breeks (which were in the car all the time), Geordie and Wull had sauntered affably by, cameras swinging. Two days later we saw ourselves in the *Scotsperson* as 'Climbers Enjoying Their Camp Fire in Glencoe'. They appeared coincident with disaster. Omens.

'Ay,' greeted Geordie.

'Ay, ay,' added Wull.

'We'll no get in yer way,' promised Geordie.

'Keep tae the side, like,' confirmed Wull, similarly stomping plumb up the middle.

On arrival, they piled arms, and Wull trod on the willow. He held out the bits, helpfully. We replaced it by another. Meanwhile Geordie had wandered down for a chat with the Apprentice.

Violent un-Doctorial oaths restored order, and silence reigned, broken only by sucking and grinding beside us as Geordie and Wull enjoyed their glacier mints. Unfortunately, a sweetie paper was spat across the foreground just as the Doctor clicked. 'It'll no be seen,' Geordie reassured us. 'Invisible,' agreed Wull.

Nevertheless the latter lumbered across to retrieve it, and coincided with the next click.

When the impossible had at last been partially achieved, we limped off exhausted. Below us, an artillery offensive traversed the panorama: Wull's rapid staccato – two from each camera, twice to make sure – and Geordie's occasional heavy clang. Angry words down at G.H.Q. indicated that they too were having trouble.

It was high time for a break. We unpacked pieces, but refreshment was diminished by the Doctor's desire to snap Mountaineers Eating and, when we were not paralysed in midbite or half-swallow, he kept crawling around us to snipe Unselfconscious Attitudes. We were almost glad to be ordered to the Great Ridge for the Action Shot.

Action Shot. I shall not recount the passionate *pas-de-deux* executed for the Action Shot. They were complex, for each of the *deux* – usually at the same time – wished to shoot the other. A sort of vertical duel.

My job was to boost the vertical bit. This entailed pulling the rope hard between them and ensuring that ironmongery did not dangle sideways or upwards. The uncooperative horizon was rigidly excluded. A hoped-for release, when the Doctor – wishing to include in his field all of pitch three – stepped backwards over the edge of pitch two, came to nothing; we hauled him back *camera intacta*. The Apprentice finally untied in a rage and stormed off, the zoom goggling to 105 in hot pursuit – 'Got him!' purred the Doctor, winding on.

Meanwhile, Geordie and Wull were busy. Geordie had his huge leather-jacketed telescopic lens – like an outsize stalker's glass – aimed at us, supported by groaning tripod and breathless Wull. He was taking an Action Shot of the Doctor taking an Action Shot of the Apprentice taking an Action Shot of the Doctor taking an Action Shot... an ever-diminishing vista easily disappearing into the maw of his monstrous monocular, a 1937 Trafalgar Mk. IV. Fortunately, its almost infinite accommodation stopped short of sound waves, which were breaking fairly blue about the Doctor's ears.

At the top he sought to mollify us. 'Can't see what you're complaining about', he sighed, 'you've taken it easy all day. I've done all the damned work....' Then he gloomily remembered he had a Funny to take, and we were allowed to descend.

At a boulder halfway down, our companion warily resurrected the subject of an Action Shot. His eyes gleamed sideways.

'Superb against that blue sky. You needn't rope up, it's only eight feet and the ground's quite soft.'

Reluctantly, the Apprentice arranged himself on a crux. 'Reach up with the right hand. Aah... *left* hand, reach *down*. Don't TOUCH anything – keep it like an *ongoing* movement: that's the impression we want. Left foot – raise it; now raise the *right* one....' Predictably, the Apprentice, following these instructions, found himself eventually quite free of the rock. It was, in fact, an off-coming movement.

He appeared in mid-air.

'Excellent! Hold it!' Click. 'Lord, I hope....'

We hurried over. No damage, only curses. A softer landing could not have been found. The Apprentice sat, stuck, in a black, amiably receptive, deer wallow. He had given one more desired impression.

'Marvellous. Stay there a moment.'

Click.

'Just the thing for the Funnies. Good man.'

Back beside the tent, apologies were still not accepted.

'... *And* the waste of an entire bloody day,' swore the Apprentice, wringing his peat-sodden doup. 'No, no; used the whole spool, all good – except for Wull and the bluebottle – some really terrific'; and the Doctor happily spun the rewinding lever.

He unclipped the back. Paused. And let out a dreadful cry.

There was nothing inside.

Empty.

The film had been left in the tent.

That distraction about the hair....

He brandished the camera, eyes and mouth at full aperture; an image of maximum aberration.

And of course just then Geordie and Wull padded by.

With ponderous agility Geordie levelled his mahogany and clanked.

His picture of our screaming group won Fourth Prize in the Funnies. It was entitled

'THE PHOTOGRAPHER:
*Who truly records with patient skill
Hours of delight upon the hill.'*   (1/30 sec., *f* 1.4).

UP THE WALL

It was the Apprentice's fault, this time. Or rather, he shared it with the Himalayas. The two of them combined to bring us a fairly nerve-cracking Saturday afternoon in one of the grimier outskirts of Edinburgh.

Before the Monsoon that year he had scaled a knife-edged pinnacle among those excitable adolescent mountains. It was a fearsome affair, beside which the Mustagh Tower and companions could have slouched unnoticed into Glen Lyon. Previous to his ascent it had been the fortress of some vague but amiable warrior-god of the snows, a putative Being adored by the simpler natives, who called it after him by a name I have preferred to forget but which could be roughly translated as Mount Lord Bonington or suchlike. It was certainly very high and very smooth, and we were proud of our companion. Mind you, he had worked for it: devotional exercises every few hours, bends, grips, pull-ups, press-ups, middle E's each weekend, evenings spent eroding Meadowbank climbing wall.... The Way to the Highest is hard.

No wonder he suffered a Reaction when he returned. No wonder he sought relief on a friend's 750 Kamikaze, a ferociously willing beast which he had unwisely exercised on the Musselburgh by-pass (the Doctor, equally fond of the occasional canter, preferred to speed on minor roads – 'twisty ones where they'd never even try to trap'). One of the two constables who booked him was an old schoolmate; the other was not. The Apprentice succeeded, nevertheless, in reducing his recorded speed by a quarter, to just under the Ton; and trying his luck further (he was still suffering from Summit Fever) had opted for Court rather than Cash. His excuse of a Following Wind appeared less and less plausible as the Case drew nearer.

His happiness was yet more diminished by the matter of Seeds. Before Expediting, he had rashly agreed with the Doctor's wife (who was one of the Sponsors) to collect on the walk-in (or in some unscrupulous bazaar) seeds of a certain Asiatic Primula which flourished in that locality. As he had several other things to do, including Mount Lord Bonington, he had decided to leave behind, lose, or suffer the theft of – he never settled on which – the (imaginary) packet containing them.

The Doctor's wife did not choose to lay the blame squarely on some erring Dhotial, and her sceptical gaze further fuelled his embarrassment. She – well versed in reducing even tougher material than the Apprentice – requested, icily sweetly, an alternative Favour:

To perform the Opening Climb on a Children's Indoor Climbing Wall at some Interdenominational Youth Arts and Activity Centre in what she was pleased to term a Deprived Area, just outside Edinburgh. Deprived or not, Craigiescunner was certainly Tough, and its children notoriously Wee Hard Men (or Women). To compound the horror, her husband had been trapped (as penance for some unimaginable misdemeanour) into Opening the Wall itself – drawing back curtains and things. For the Doctor's wife was a Trustee of this Centre and determined to display both an Eminent Professional Man and a Distinguished Himalayan Mountaineer doing their stuff before the Deprived. A third exhibit was another Trustee, Sir Angus McFell, exemplifying the Successful Entrepreneur and Local Politician; who was to make the opening Speech, and really rub in the salt. Loyal as the Apprentice is, he might well have caught flu just before that Saturday, had not Sir Angus turned out to be the magistrate hearing his case the week after; the Following Wind might therefore pick up, a little.

My companions of so many difficult days implored me to see them through this one. So when it came, all three of us slipped in by a back door. The Trustees, local councillors, the odd minister and a battery of priests festered about the front entrance, awaiting Sir Angus. We knew him only by repute: he had sprung originally from some tourist trap at Taynuilt, and expanded deviously enough to become a well-known Contractor. One of his enterprises, Kruachan KonKrete-Krushers plc, had masticated much of the Old Towns of the Central Belt, and the products of another, Etive Slabs plc, were employed by flutterings of architects to pave square miles of New ones: at an ankle-wrenching and slippery gradient whose multiform cracks alone prevented pedestrians from gliding to destruction. Sir Angus distributed his gains skilfully enough for a grateful Government to award him a knighthood, and a struggling new University an Honorary Doctorate – which in pre-metric days would have been an L.S.D.

We awaited himself and his speech with interest, and meanwhile mooched about inside. The corridor leading to the main hall was lined with tables displaying the Arts – scrawls and daubs indicative of undoubted if unspecified *joie-de-vivre*, and a few hundredweight of much more particularised statuary, in some quick-set plastic substance. These arrested the wandering eye. Behind the Mickey Mice, Wally Dugs, St. Christophers, B.V.M.'s and Seven Dwarfs, some outstandingly virile Apollos raised themselves, partnered by topless – but certainly not bottomless – Aphrodites. Many outstripped the outrageous, and clearly had been smuggled in uncensored. The children of Craigiescunner were a worldly bunch. A collection of busts amused us too – of pop stars, the Pope, and well-hated (unidenominational) politicians; two of us being further diverted by a lifelike Head of the Doctor: who complained that the nose and chin, especially, 'verged on caricature'.... Still, it was Thoughtful of them.

In the Main Hall itself, normally devoted to various tiresome forms of Activity, sat serried rows of young and their putative progenitors. Through the industrious haze of tobacco fug we recognised the Dais – chairs, table, jug of water, glasses: behind that, a white sheet covering, presumably, the Children's Climbing Wall. Ropes, harnesses, No Smoking notices, hung from above; a huge mattress lay on the floor.

To deafening hoots, cheers and boos, the Entrance Party arrived and marched up to the Dais. Sir Angus led, bovine, redfaced, with a white-toothed and determined grin, wiping his gleaming brow from perspiration and a rain of wet pellets that had met him at the door. My companions edged in behind them. The Doctor's wife crystallised for us a granitic smile, and elegantly folded her intimidating stature up there at the back. I squatted in front of the audience, among fag-ends.

Some nondenominational nonentity, the Chairman of the Trust, introduced Sir Angus; who charged at his speech without ado, bellowing his audience into silent admiration. His peanut-butter vowels and milk-pudding consonants – the Conceived Pronunciation of Lord Provosts on the Southern make – spattered forth with a vigour and velocity rare in such usually lip-lickingly uncertain linguists. Frequently he tugged at his collar to ease the strain.

This was a Claimbing Wall. To teach you to Claimb. Claimbers claimbed rocks and mountains, but they all began on a Claimbing Wall, laike this. (The Distinguished Himalayan Mountaineer choked, but was silenced by a deft kick from the Eminent Professional Man). They conquered the Haighest Mountains by skills learnt on a Wall-laike-this - care, *care*, planning and *making sure*. So that Nothing goes wrong. Thought Out. Planned. But also by Qualities brought out in you – YOU – by a Wall-laike-this: Courage, Will-Power, Determination to take a Risk. He thundered on, demolishing difficulties and logic like a well-serviced bulldozer. 'What you will learn from a Wall-like-this, is how to be a Success in Life. *Really* to Claimb. To claimb the Real Things. To Master. Not to graipe and grovel, but to be Men'; ('or Women,' he granted). The male parent among whose ash I sat, bent down and nudged me: 'Ah'd no like tae work fer yon bastard – eh?'; and spat meaningly. 'A Wall-laike-this...' and so on for five more minutes, by which time most of us – perhaps even my expectorant neighbour – became convinced that a spontaneously calculated, prudently daredevil Ascent of a Wall-laike-this must inevitably raise us to high executive altitude in concerns like Kruachan KonKrete-Krushers plc and Etive Slabs, plc. Great.

He stopped suddenly, extended an arm to the startled Doctor, and roared: 'I declare this Children's Indoor Claimbing Wall at Craigiescunner Interdenominational Youth Arts and Activity Centre – OPEN!'

He swung towards the sheet. We all gaped, mesmerised. The Doctor jumped up, couped his chair (the Apprentice, in his best move that day, grabbed it), and marched to the dangling rope. He pulled.

Nothing happened. 'Not that one, ass!' hissed his spouse, 'the red one, with a tassel on it!'

He marched across, amid rapturous applause, and pulled that.

The curtain parted in the centre and drew back, jerkily, revealing the Wall-laike-this.

It much resembled the usual climbing wall, except that it was bright green, with pink holds, and on a smaller scale; and that in the middle was stuck a large white poster which announced:

Bloody McFell
Done himself well

followed by two quite unquotable lines, the whole a quatrain rhyming *a a b a* and evidently a product of the Post-Modern Literature class.

A Trustee rose hastily and tore it down, to further cheering. Now it was the Apprentice's turn. He pushed back his chair and approached the Wall. The Doctor buckled him into his harness (it was a tight fit), whispered 'Don't make it look too easy,' backed away, and held the

(correct) rope. Sir Angus, at a slightly higher pitch and with more spittle, broadcast his commentary on all this. It was wildly inaccurate, but went down well. Paper darts, plastic cups, old syringes, flew in a friendly manner towards him.

'Now on a Mountain if he fell, he would be dashed thousands of feet into thousands of pieces. Here he would land on this mattress,' (kicking it). 'But he won't fall, he can't fall, he has claimbed great Himalayan monsters, he has just come back, he is one of our Fainest Young Claimbers, *you* can be laike him, he goes up and up, *carefully* – see – but never hesitating, he is quaite safe, you will be quaite safe, look how the rope goes over the pulley and down to his Steady Companion, the Doctor here.' Sir Angus crossed to the Doctor, planted a large incorporating arm about him and beamed at the hooting and cheering throng, patting his beautifully-dressed iron-grey hair in satisfaction.

The Apprentice poised momentarily, and surveyed the top few feet. There seemed to be chalk on these last holds. Jug-handles; they didn't need chalk. Stung by shouts of 'Gerronupit, Jessie!' he seized them and heaved towards the ceiling.

But: the chalk was not chalk. It was that quick-setting modelling plastic. The jug-handles snapped off neatly, as presumably planned, and the Distinguished Himalayan Mountaineer plunged all of ten feet on to the mattress.

Bounce; bounce; roll.

His Steady Companion, engrossed in conversation within the circumference of Sir Angus and taken unawares, was shot upwards a couple of feet, his elbow on the way smiting that worthy in his (redeemable) City of London teeth; the rope which, alas, he had held so steadily, whipped around to wrap them both intimately together. It also dislodged Sir Angus' unsuspected iron-grey wig.

There was no doubt that the Opening was, for the Deprived at any rate, a huge success. Their long-sustained appreciation loosened quite a few ceiling tiles. Then, overwhelming the demoralised rabble on the Dais, everyone rushed to try and claimb the Wall. West Berlin might have twinkled the other side. A special route was cleared for the Doctor – no false handles, they assured him. He had difficulty shortening himself into the under-age holds, but thereafter swarmed up in some style until, at the final mantelshelf, he forgot it was a Children's Wall and his six feet two smote the ceiling, bringing down, appositely enough, part of a plastic cornice. Again immense applause; during which we delicately vanished through the side door again. I overtook my old neighbour. He coughed out a fag, back-handed his mouth and sputtered delightedly: 'Man, that was a grand do, eh? Bloody McFell, Done himsel well....' The rest dispersed itself into bursts of bronchial hilarity and generous spitting over open sights. We fled.

That evening, as we thrashed sweatily through steely Sitka spruce in the rain with rucksacks and tent on the way to a secluded upper corrie, the Doctor, detaching himself from some grinning coniferous entanglement, saw fit to observe that 'Some people, you know, develop a kind of passion for Climbing Walls. Sir Angus, for instance. But I don't envy them – they do everything indoors; you know, they just wouldn't enjoy this kind of thing, one little bit.'

A WIDER VIEW

No, we are not really skiers. We agree with Unna that skiers regard a mountain as a thing to use skis on; self-righteous mountaineers like ourselves regard skis as just one more thing to use (or not use) on a mountain. The wider view.

And use not only by ski-touring over the backsides of sleeping beasties on a Haute Route, but also by climbing their rudely-awakened faces, with skis there to rub it in. A really wide view.

This last ideal of ski-mountaineering proved elusive. We had frequently skied up to a difficult winter climb; left them at the bottom; climbed it; roped down; and after searching frantically in the dark, never found our skis again and been forced to walk back for them next morning. Or, we had skied to an easy climb and hoped to crown it by skiing blissfully down from the summit, either through (*a*) climbing with skis on our backs or (*b*) towing them behind us; (*a*) effectively swept chimneys up to the first bend, (*b*) grievously eroded both skis and whatever steps we tried to descend after untangling them. Then we arranged for a Tame Friend with skins to drag our skis up to the summit by gentle slopes while we climbed by a decent route. But naturally if a Friend is as Tame as that he must also be stupid; and never did he find the summit or the top of our climb, even without the usual mist, but wandered around hallooing disconsolately for hours, causing us also to halloo and trail about, and eventually to plowter down on foot through cursing miles of breakable crust; arriving himself, exhausted and weeping, about midnight, with a claque of rebellious planks yelping and snapping at his ankles, loyally losing only an odd stick or bit of Tyrolia on the way.

Last weekend, though, everything had worked. We dumped skis below Raeburn's Gully on Lochnagar, climbed it by The Gutter, glissaded what was left of the left-hand branch of the Black Spout and skied back to the car. A gentlemanly excursion which even the Apprentice confessed was satisfying.

This weekend, conditions promised sterner stuff and we planned Parallel B, which the Doctor deemed worthy of his new front-pointers.

But Saturday blizzards blocked all roads in that direction. In any direction – Dalnaspidal, Glen Ogle, you name it. So, in outrageously fine Sunday weather we finished up on the main road between Crieff and Comrie, at a recently-cleared patch by some cottages, whose occupants let us park beside another skiers' vehicle, likewise snowed out from accustomed haunts. We enlarged the patch with the Doctor's shovel and calmed the old Merc – which had wallowed like a panic-stricken mastiff – with the tightest of chains. Then we set off simply to tour the foothills of Ben Chonzie, which were extremely proud of their dazzling new status. They swelled with ultra-violet. Moreover, in an easterly wind, the Doctor assured us, we should continually inhale Glen Turret, from its distillery over the shoulder.

We soon left the other tracks along the forestry road and struck bare slopes. Fine buxom-breasted snowy virgins they were, billowing into the azure. We skinned on, in delicious silky rhythm. Snow and silence stretched unbroken. Dream-like.

Then a faint chirrupy squeak.

'Hush!' from the Doctor. We all stopped.

We listened.

Silence.

'I bet that was a Snow Bunting,' he breathed, excitedly. We groaned, for he had suffered from ornithology already that season. So much so that the Apprentice and I had thoughts of subscribing to something like the Royal Society for the Prevention of Birds, or whatever. 'Hush!'

Silence.

'We've scared it. They're so suspicious. Don't like people, you know. It's the blizzard that's brought them so low.' Indeed. We moved off.

Squeak. Chirrup.

Halt again. 'Yes, a snow bunting – that curious hesitant modest little song. Delightful wee mites. And as you see, invisible against the snow....' Etc., etc. The serenade ceased abruptly when we stopped, resumed as we moved on ('Oho, they're *clever*!'). The Apprentice, of a cold logical mind, held me back with him as the Doctor pushed ahead. Chirrup, chirrup. It only sang when the Doctor moved, only stopped when he stopped.

We informed him it was not *Plectrophenax nivalis* but a once common, now much rarer, visitant to Scottish snowslopes – The Little Squeaking

Ski-Strap. A haunter of old-fashioned bindings.

The Doctor seemed hurt. He wrapped himself in his Extra Years. 'You young chaps are too narrow-minded, obsessive, selfish. You should make allowance for maturer people's naturally greater range of interests.' For the next hundred feet, he illustrated his thesis by dreadful examples of youthful prodigies like Wee Dander or That Boy who abandoned us below the Aonach Eagach. 'You should take a Wider View....'

Then we breasted a rise, and saw the owners of the roadside ski-tracks.

Two figures, short and tall, watching a small third one pirouetting high up.

We sighed. You can't avoid meeting people these days. Poor *Plectrophenax.*

We reached them. A large mournful-looking man with a grizzled moustache, and a small bright boy. They'd gone far enough. Just beginners. The lad had sprained his knee, anyway; he cursed his luck colourfully. 'Na, na, come awa doon, Wullie', said the man, 'it's a long way back.'

'Hey!' whistled Willie as the small figure above coruscated an untidy melodrama of turns. 'Braw, eh?'

'Pretty good for his age,' agreed the unwary Doctor. 'Wunnerful, considerin,' confirmed the elderly man, 'but bloody stupid all the same, never left off all day. An he smokes like a fish, tae.' 'Shouldn't smoke at *his* age,' warned the Doctor, stepping deeper into a mire, 'after thirty more years he'll be gey short of breath.' 'He will that,' said the man, 'noo, Wullie, awa doon an we'll wait for him at the car; ye can be playin yer new tapes, mind, there.'

The Doctor patted the small irate head benignly. 'Yes, you take your father's good advice.' We nodded.

The head looked up indignantly.

'He's no ma feyther.' Pointing to the figure above, now herring-boning determinedly back again: '*He's* ma feyther!'

We should have minded our own business. But worse was to come. The large man rubbed his sleeve across his nose, and turned to go. 'Aye, an he's *mine*, tae, begod,' he sourly observed. 'Awa doon wi ye, Wullie. Pap'll be back in his ain time, as per bluidy usual. Us weans dinnae count.'

They were about to shuffle down when the stricken Apprentice was further struck: 'That's no Peerie Bob Peterson, is it?' he demanded.

It was Peerie Bob Peterson. A legendary figure in the West, Peerie Bob had scrambled about the cliffs of his (so he said) native Shetland Lord knows how many years ago, then gone – or been ejected – to Glasgow and into uncountable jobs, pubs and horrendous climbing escapades, none exactly – or often even remotely – to his credit. His first wife – mother of our large dour acquaintance – fled to New York for a quiet life, and in his reputedly seventieth year he had reputedly married Willie's mother (a real flash cookie) and, between other V.S.s, begotten Willie. Now, beginning to feel his age, he had taken to skiing.

We said our farewells and plugged on, vastly intrigued. Peerie Bob swept down to us in a cloud of spray and tobacco smoke. He spat out a fag-end.

He reached our shoulders, the Doctor's waist-band. Beneath his bright orange balaclava, black rat-lively eyes sniffed us. A red morocco countenance, thin twitching shrew-nose, long white tucked-away baccy-stained whiskers (grown every winter for whatever resorts give free chair-lifts to O.A.P.s), and three or four well-distributed yellow teeth.

Hardly the typical Shetlander. His genes must have blown there on some strong southwesterly gale. His voice, too, had lost – if it ever possessed – those reassuringly rocksolid consonants and Muckle Flugga vowels. It exhibited a disarmingly Glaswegian agility.

'Whaurs youse boys gaun?'

We vaguely indicated up the corrie.

'I'll join youse. O.K.? I'm aye for company, ken.'

Fine. We all four continued, Peerie Bob herring-boning the steep bits. But no more silence. And an enveloping fug like the toilet outside a No Smoking compartment. We yearned for those promised whiffs of delicate distillery-emitted Glen Turret.

Peerie Bob recounted endlessly improbable yarns, well dosed with personal heroics ('If it hadna been fer me...'). And proudly bemoaned his advanced years. 'Eighty-five, ken!' Nonsense; but he was no chicken. Beside him, we two and the Doctor warmed into contemporaries.

He confessed he yearned for a climb. His old companions were 'aa deid' – few of them, we suspected, from their beds, if they'd climbed often with him; and the young yins nowadays too Academic (a fine catarrhal contempt) and Safety Conscious (a terminally bronchial dismissal). He rolled fag after fag during this with no slackening of rhythm, he plucked paper and tobacco from the surrounding air, rolled them, licked them and lit them, blethering all the while. He liked a good simple climb, with just that bit of Risk (eh?) that gave it Interest. Remembering the multitude of disasters Peerie Bob had thriven on, we shuddered and blessed our present innocent slopes. But not for long.

'Aye, just like yon!' A ski-stick pointed. Yon was a sudden small black defile soiling a spotless upper corrie on our left. 'Bet, noo, it's never been done! Too easy in summer. Jist dandy the day – a bit o Interest... eh?' He slowed and gazed at us appealingly, little ferret eyes suddenly round with liquid simplicity.

We were annoyed at the disturbance of our day; and for feeling annoyed. A lonely old man. Shame.

'Would you, would you like to, have a look at it with us?' hazarded the kindly Doctor, heedless of previous omens. 'Would I no!' Ah, he was, despite all slanders, a true enthusiast. Poor old sod. We thawed; we skinned up and planted skis firmly below this little gully, marking the site (from bitter experience) by a big snow cairn. Peerie Bob penguined further on his absurdly short skis and stashed them under a boulder.

Then he let fly a 'Hurroo!' and began to squirrel up the flour, wielding a ski-stick and a small terrordactyl plucked from his bulging rucksack. The latter aid we thought excessive for such an apparent Grade I. Ourselves, we possessed the Doctor's inevitable axe, his tricounis, 50 feet of line and two ski-sticks. Ample. We two wore dual-purpose double-priced ski-mountaineering boots, Peerie Bob something – from years of misuse – approaching them in unsuitability for either pursuit. 'We can tow the old goat down when he crashes out,' remarked the Apprentice charitably. 'Thing is, keep out of his way till then.'

We followed the blazed groove into steep hard steps. Above us a flailing of weapons and untunefully improper carolling. Peerie Bob was happy. 'Does you good to hear him busy again!' cooed the Doctor, whose knowledge of snow buntings and Bob seemed on a par.

Icicly rock closed in on us. The gully narrowed to a slit and steepened to a cornice. A glance downwards brought out our emergency line. Peerie Bob coughed scorn. 'A doddle!' he spat, contemptuously curling his smoke.

Doddle or not, the Apprentice swam up and tied him on. Whatever his real age, he was too old to keep at this pace and, small as he might be, we preferred him on a string when he eventually had to fall out. The Doctor, plus axe, became his solicitous second and kicked scrabbles into steps. Peerie Bob imperiously threw him down the ski-stick – 'Nae room!' Our youthful companion collected it obediently.

We were nearly at the top of this increasingly exacting slot when it narrowed to a mere chimney cleaving holdless white-ice walls. The terrordactyl and its owner sang in happy discord, between scrambling silences and blue exhaust smoke. We, of normal human stature, regarded this final pitch – a slot like a mini-Parallel B – with horror. At his age! On bald tyres!

Peerie Bob was deaf to entreaties. Slabbering, skiting, coughing and clutching, he wormed up to the very top of the rock slit – a wide crack as holdless as the ice all round – and there indulged in, of all things, a back-and-knee job....

We dug in our anguished axe and constructed a Forth Bridge erection with ski-sticks; and waited in terror.

A note of alarm above. We grabbed the thread of line – it would fillet our fingers, for sure.

Nothing, nobody, fell.

'I'm stuck!' he cried. 'Jammed! Canna move!'

He roared with most disconcerting laughter, a paroxysm which probably settled him in even more securely.

'It's ma heuks! It's ma heuks!' Chokes and guffaws.

We looked at each other. Heuks?! Sheer senility.... No place to laugh in, here. How could we get him down, or ourselves up? Humour the old fool. The strain had been too much.

The Doctor leant out and called comfortingly up the flue in his best chimneyside manner. He was genially rebuffed. Peerie Bob was rock-firm, and would haul us all up to him. After that –

'You jist climb on owre me. *I'm* the only holds here. I'm a right good chockiestane.'

Chockiestane, though perilous, sounded healthier than chuckiestane so one by one, reluctantly accepting well-pensioned assistance, we gingerly processed over a hilarious Peerie Bob, the Doctor leading and placing his tricounis with therapeutic exactitude in a kind of multiple acupuncture. The Apprentice trod as hard as he could; to press him in.

It certainly was an unusual pitch, exceedingly aromatic; Peerie Bob's attire being coeval with himself, and his baccy almost as strong.

These intimacies over, we three belayed under the cornice. The Apprentice hung down and persuaded our aged companion free of western Perthshire with his boot.

Wearily, we turned to the cornice. It impended unforgivingly. As Peerie Bob crawled stiffly up to us, we heard ominous cracks and grindings. The Doctor called out and leapt aside, searching for tell-tale fissures above. 'Hush!' he cried, ears cocked.

'It's only ma knees, lads. They get awfy bad in the cauld. But – it's a grand cornice. Nae bother at aa.' He crept crepitatingly past us. The Lesser Creaking Knee-Cap, we informed the unsmiling Doctor.

We held him on a tight rein and let him thresh with terrordactyl and ski-stick, dislodging it seemed acres of snowcake. Then propelled him up the funnel he'd excavated.

The sun shone through, and he was on top, capering and shouting more rude songs. A revolting old creature. He untied and disappeared, leaving us to struggle up on our own. We recalled a similar desertion by the boy prodigy. 'Only Climb With Those Of Your Own Age,' hissed the Doctor through snow.

But it was nice up there. Then we all set off down to the skis. For a good run back on boards.

We plunged away, rejoicing in limbs once more. Peerie Bob lagged behind. Our consciences again. Poor old devil; if we felt stiff, what about him, vile as he might be? Heavens, here he was, running down backwards, fast enough, taking quick looks into his left hand.

He explained that his knees always seized up on the descent, unless he faced backwards and fooled his arthritic joints into thinking they were still going uphill.

'I can bash on aa day uphill, mind. It's the doonhill that gets ye when ye're auld.' (The Doctor later admitted, uneasily, that this was indeed so). We were impressed; most of all by his little driving mirror. It was cracked – from the Apprentice's boot earlier – 'but the wife's plenty mair.'

The slope steepened to the corrie. A fine sitting glissade: but too deep and slow – we three, poling desperately, could only ooze downward.

Then a swish and a roar, and a triumphal cry. Peerie Bob shot past, at terrifying speed. He was light, did not sink, and skimmed on a plastic agricultural sack (N:15, P:15, K:21, with added Magnesium). Far too fast. There were boulders down there!

'Old fool! He's done it this time! Have to carry him back after all!' The Apprentice seemed cheered by the thought.

The geriatric dot below us, heading straight for disaster, leant backwards and disappeared in a cloud of snow. Which settled, revealing Peerie Bob sitting unscathed, grinning and rolling a fag a few feet from a vast glacial erratic, cheated of its prey.

When we arrived, he was inhaling complacently.

'Ma heuks, see? The verra thing when ye're an auld man. Davy Glen gave me them years ago.'

A harness, bristling behind with curved iron hooks. 'Ye lean back – an ye stop. Jist as good on grass. Grand on Suilven.... Saves ma knees no end.'

We'd heard of Davy Glen and his larks with the Dargies; the Doctor, of course, had even seen him. We regarded Bob with increasing respect. The Experience of Age. He certainly took a refreshingly wide view of things. Made us feel stodgy, safe, suburban; naive....

To hell with respect! Where were our skis? Our snow cairn had vanished, replaced by a mighty cone fed from Peerie Bob's wanton demolition of the cornice, and from all the loose snow it had swept down.... Buried, lost, lost till the spring!

Peerie Bob nodded in sympathy. 'That's terrible. Ye should always put them oot o the way o a gully slide, boys.' He extracted his own from under the boulder, and smartly clicked them on. 'Ye'll no have a shuffle, either?'

No, but there was one in the car. Och, he'd ski down and fetch it up. Och, his knees were fine on skis. It was the walking that did them in at the end of a good day; at his age, like. Skis was nae bother. 'Jist ye wait, lads. No lang.'

And he slipped off, rolling a fag expertly between linked turns.

Of course, he never did come back. This being predicted by the Apprentice, we grimly set about disinterring our transport. An hour of the Doctor's axe, plus his dissecting skills, uncovered all our skis and most of the sticks. Enough.

In the gathering dusk we hissed away, frozen and muttering. At the

road we met a large party, with lamps, ropes, stretchers. We guessed immediately, having been sustained all the way by the Apprentice's uncharitable stories of Peerie Bob. That old scoundrel had ordered a Rescue Party, and this very minute, a Hero, would be conducting Press Interviews – for Gold! Free drinks had already flowed through the whiskers.... Maturer people, the Doctor had warned us, possessed a naturally greater range of interests. A wider view.

We stormed into the throng, blazing. A cottage door opened and a small figure sped through into a car, which drove off hurriedly. A bottle was flung out. We glimpsed the morose Elder Brother at the wheel, Feyther crouched in cover beside him, and a cheerful brat at the back window.

The Doctor in righteous wrath is overwhelming, and his doubtless unethical descriptions of Senile Delusion mollified the rescue team and also – together with impressively legal jargon – rooted out whatever press contacts Peerie Bob had 'phoned from the cottage, and stunned those gentlemen to unaccustomed silence.

So that the whole episode was reduced to one small paragraph in an obscure Gallovidian evening paper, and the price of a half-day ticket for Peerie Bob on Aònach Mor the next weekend. When, we were glad to see, it rained heavily from Friday to Monday.

Of course, that kept us off Parallel B.

But we took a wider view.

FAMILY MATTERS

'Families and climbing simply do not mix,' the Doctor had pronounced. 'It's bad enough managing ropes – without apron strings, umbilical cords and matrimonial chains. We come here to get away from all that.' The Apprentice had said he agreed thoroughly, and peered up at the next pitch. I myself felt a few reservations (we also came here so we could – eventually – get back to all that), but not many. Certainly, no one could approve of people like the Oliphants – who shamelessly displayed outbursts of babies all across the Highlands. 'Sandy's changed nappies in front of nearly every damned Club Hut,' the Doctor exclaimed indignantly. We felt uncomfortable beside such milk-bespattered exhibitionists.

Like most of those we met on the hill, we knew little, and cared less, about each other's domestic concerns. (Imagine a Mrs. Geordie, a Mrs. Wull – the latter presumably in duplicate....) The Apprentice and I had visited the Doctor's house a few times, and enjoyed wonderful banquets there; but his children were always away, and his wife – well, we have mentioned her elsewhere; kindly, indeed, but – for us – about as approachable as Nanda Devi, whose remote high-nebbit elegance she shared. Doubtless the Doctor enjoyed a warmer relationship – they sparred conversationally with mutual entertainment – but we preferred to keep a safe distance from that imposing Face, especially when presenting a Southern aspect. Of the Apprentice's family life, neither the Doctor nor I knew anything. He did exhibit an occasional passing weakness for girl-friends – or just girls; but apart from such pardonable peccadilloes in a lad less than half the Doctor's age, and a good four years younger than myself, we climbed happily among – and with – all four sexes, our mountains unperturbed by tornadoes from any domestic teapot. The Apprentice, indeed, boasted a tough unconcern for all family matters. He agreed thoroughly with the Doctor, and hauled himself over the crux.

Hence our astonishment when, after several weekends of his 'being too busy to join us', we came across him one evening at Traprain with what the Doctor nostalgically described as a 'a right wee smasher'. To our pointedly innocent remarks, he mumbled conventionally red-faced replies. He was teaching Jeanie to climb rock – not that she needed much tuition, she swarmed up: you could well say, beautifully. We – I certainly – envied him. Small, flashing-eyed, with a most attractive smile. The Doctor and I became maudlin, drinking lonely toasts in Daddy McKay's: for the Apprentice would spend even our Thursday evenings with her on some climbing wall. The Doctor dolefully predicted an outcome of Oliphantiasis.

Things did look serious. Not only for the peace of mind of our companion but, more importantly, for ourselves. Hills would not be the same without the Apprentice. Imagine our surprise, therefore, at his behaviour when we next saw him with Jeanie.

This was at Craig-y-Barns – the weather being too wet for further north. They were talking to a tall, handsome (I suppose) fairhaired guy; and then this guy pinched Jeanie's arm affectionately; and bolted up the rock after her, in the approved biological pursuit. And the Apprentice looked on, coolly; even with satisfaction.

He came shyly towards us. He pointed at his lost love, now two free pitches ahead of her admirer, and said: 'See that! I taught her no bad after all, eh?'

'Taught her to go off with somebody else?!' we exclaimed. 'Sure. Shug's been hot on her for months, and Jeanie on him. But it was nearly all over. She couldn't share his climbs at weekends. Now she can – and is she chuffed! Never look back any more.'

This unlikely philanthropy was rationally explained, it turned out, by Jeanie being the Apprentice's kid sister. Yet I felt puzzled, as well as sour, that his thoughtfulness extended to that yob Shug. But he had a good reason. It strolled up just then in the highly-powered form of another young lady. The Apprentice blushed and stammered. This was Cat, Catherine, the sister of Shug, and one of the top climbers of the year. The Apprentice was sweet on Cat. It was therefore politic to be sweet to Shug. Love my Cat, love me. That lady did not appear likely to be sweet on anyone; but had, it seems, climbed a few times with the Apprentice. She purred dangerously at him. Jaguar rather than Cat. We backed away from our perspiring companion, and left him to field her barely-suppressed energies.

Then the delightful Jeanie and the cursed Shug came down. 'Okay, Hughie?' grinned Cat, 'satisfied now?' A foursome was speedily arranged on a fairly Extending area of the crag. Shug and Jeanie set off, then Cat and her Apprentice.

Now the Apprentice is very good on extending rock. Very good indeed. But Cat stormed ahead, a ripple of tiger-skin; and so demoralised him he began to slow down and grab at things. Shug, really no bad climber at all, blast him, lost Jeanie in the slipstream of Cat. The two girls hooted, made rude signs, and raced off to the next Tier.

Shug and the Apprentice, one blown, the other disgruntled, slithered down to us.

'Hell, you've taught Jeanie a thing or two,' gasped Shug admiringly, mopping his brow. 'Cat's going to take her on a new route she's made.'

The Apprentice looked bitter. '*Womans' Lib*, I bet she'll call it,' he growled. He enjoyed an evidently stormy relationship with Her Felinity, and this was not one of the Good Days.

The Doctor tried to be helpful. 'You know, girls are likely to climb better than us on these balance routes, at that age; less frustration, less rage, they take it more smoothly.' He quailed under six hostile eyes. 'Up to a certain time that is,' he added. 'Until, in fact, they've had a baby. That slows 'em down – physically and mentally. Makes 'em more responsible. Good thing, too,' he whispered, glancing about him with understandable caution.

'Doesn't seem to have affected Cat,' remarked Shug, off-handedly.

The Apprentice stared at him, horror-struck.

Shug looked surprised at his concern, and added, 'Wee Jerry'll be a year in August. You havena seen him? Cat didna tell you? His Granny's fair daft on him, he aye stays with her. Cat's fond of him, like, sees him now and again. But it's the rocks she's after – an no the ones you give the cradle, eh?' He cackled at his stupid joke and scanned the cliff.

We waited for further information. The Apprentice licked dry lips. There might still be hope.

'She's no married? She never – .'

'Och no, of course not. What an idea. No yet, anyway. God, look at what they're doing – pheeeew....' Shug's mouth fell open.

The Apprentice ignored the climbing. He remained fixed on family matters.

'The... the... Father.... Is *he* interested?'

'In climbing?'

'No, for _____ sake! In the baby!'

'Interested? Oh aye. Jeeze, look at that. Jeanie, girl, Jeanie.... O aye. Sep's real delighted. Keeps sending presents for him near every week. What a move – did you see that? Jeeze....'

Sep? The name alarmed our bells. We suddenly recalled meeting, a year before at these very crags, Virginia Prusik – that small intensely knotted American rock-scorpion from Joshua Tree – and her amply-flowing pink companion, the genial Sep....

'Is he American?' The Apprentice sounded hoarse.

'American? O aye. Cat's likely gaun out there inside the year. She'll be havin to take the bairn along with her – Sep's as fond of it as she is of him. She'll be for Yosemite and yon places. But she'll have to pay her fare, ken: Sep's folks want an old-fashioned-like Ohio wedding. And Sep's a real soft family-man sort of a guy, he'll no disappoint them. You've met him?' he asked the by-now tragic Apprentice. 'Cat's not told you? Ah, she's a real hard case, Cat, no time for anything but climbing; don't think her family matters much to her nowadays. No ties. She keeps us all at arm's length. No like your Jeanie....'

Shrieks and whistles. The girls were coming down, and our informative conversation ended.

'It's no use,' explained the Doctor, peering into the mirror as we joined the A9, 'families and climbing simply don't mix.'

We two remained silent. The Apprentice's silence suggested he agreed – thoroughly. My own was occupied by imagining how perhaps I might call on him at his house some evening – Shug being away, of course; preferably in America, married to Sep's sister.

AN ARTICLE OF FAITH

The Doctor is a persistent man, loyal to his beliefs. Two or three years ago he led us up a winter route on some vegetatious horror we encountered in the West, a loose and rambling sniff-about, which he followed remorselessly to its top end across a mutually disagreeing rubble of rock and slush. As route-finding, if not climbing, it was epic enough and he insisted that his peregrination be recorded for the benefit of whatever Posterity might visit that god-forsaken area. So he scribbled notes on 'The Solution', as he rashly christened it, in the tent that night. 'A good Grade III; must go in the next *Journal*!'

Things intervened and when he looked out his scribblings again he discovered one page – describing the final, crux, pitch – was missing. 'Dropped out of the file! Been shredded!'

He must go back and reinvestigate that pitch. Accuracy, he maintained, is essential in descriptions of new climbs: slovenliness betrays the faith of our successors. Each one of those bald stereotyped paragraphs defacing so many pages of so many journals is a Scientific Communication: inexorably boring to the casual reader, but of prodigious, obsessive, interest to any would-be explorer of those particular few square metres. 'It's Reporting an Experiment: you can prove it true or false by simply repeating the described process. Testable topographical research! Not like Munro-ticking – if you cheat there, only your Recording Angel suffers; but a New Climb is up for public adjudication. One just has to be Exact!'

We sympathised. It is a human weakness to like your name in print, at the head of a fine new route as much as at the foot of a list of Munroists. And not a selfish one – journal editors, guidebook compilers, publishers, printers, booksellers, depend on it for bread.

But we refused to waste a good winter on so scavenging an expedition. It was therefore some time before we took up The Solution again. Naturally, on a driech drizzly thawing weekend fit for nothing else.

We peered about below the cliff. According to those Doctorial notes still existing (though not to non-Doctorial recollections), *The route is unmistakable – a striking direct line immediately obvious on sighting the crag.*

Somewhere. Somewhere....

We identified the start of the climb only when the Apprentice recognised his old spare sock, left behind at our beginning the year before. Somewhat holey, faded and shrunk, fit only for a one-legged dwarf, but a topological certainty. Fresh pieces of fallen rock lay about it.

Above it, pitch one. *A clean corner bounding the lowest buttress on the E.* The buttress presumably being that part of the snowy gravel a little steeper than the angle of rest, the corner three sharpish stones in line above each other; and time, sheer time, must have grown that grimy beard of lichen all over them.

We kitted up. Small stones fell around us. A striking route, indeed... The Apprentice, as so often, offered the Doctor his spare helmet. The Doctor swore by his own thick fishing hat: 'Helmets are damned dangerous; with hats, you keep alert, hear more.' But he donned the dome to please us; and within a minute let fly an oath. A pebble pinged from his helmet. 'You see!' he cried, snatching it off and replacing the hat, 'damned dangerous: on only a minute, and hit by a stone!'

The experiment was irrefutable. Be faithful to your own beliefs. We began to go up, embarking on a long meander that did not end for weeks.

The Doctor led, notes round his neck. Once again we trod the watery glue of wet ice. 'Purely a winter climb,' its originator observed. He followed his Description as far as possible, though a few minor landmarks – the tilting flake, the uneasy block – had shifted downhill a bit, to left or right. The notes were eagerly readjusted, with no sense of scientific shame. 'A winter climb is, after all, constantly changing....'

Astonishingly, he did ferret out his approximately original route. The crux, though, remained in cloud above. We reached the pitch below it: *A large smooth slab, climbed by ice on its W.* No ice today; and the slab was split by a huge fresh crack. Yet this seemed the place: damn-all either side....

The Doctor scrawled another amendment, put away his notes and gallantly essayed the slab by its newly-inviting crack. As he grabbed its edges it quivered, wobbled wider; a horrid rumble underfoot....

'Weathering!' averred the Doctor, mounting it nimbly nevertheless.

He vanished beneath the hem of the cloud.

Then, a shout. As from the old Tay Bridge.

'It's gone...! Not here any more!'

The cloud was obligingly lifted higher by the Creator of the Problem whose Solution we had embarked upon.

Our companion then appeared, poised on the rim of an airy rip-off: a fearsome gash beneath him in front; and, overhanging above, far out of reach, a ghastly white scar glaring from the otherwise melancholy cliff.

There *was* no final pitch any more. Weathering. The carefully-described wall, like its documentation, had dropped out of the file; been shredded.

To proceed was Impossible, Unjustifiable. Everything shook, ourselves especially. We held him by pressed-in runners, but his feline skills sufficed, and we all scuttled down, the Apprentice, as anchorman, soothing an increasingly restive mountain.

At the bottom, a fresh heap of debris, burying the sock. The spare helmet had been dented. 'You see – these things *attract* stonefall! Damned dangerous.' Small bits still fell about us, remnants – or precursors. But he had to photograph the loss of his last pitch.

Then off to the car, followed by ruminations of rockery. We never looked back.

The Doctor took his bereavement manfully. But it did pose an ethical problem. You can't publish a description of a route that no longer exists. Science would be outraged; no re-run is possible. Yet that last pitch *had* been so exciting. People *would* be interested to read about it.

So he must redesign his communication as a Personal Account of the whole climb – before and after. Certainly the *Journal* Editor would publish an article of such unusual interest. 'A most discerning man, James Anderson. Prefers historical accounts. Detests the superficial and trivial. Very strict about facts. Should be more editors like that. Knew him, anyway, at school.' We two thought that Editor a self-important Pain: aye pontificating about the Spirit of Mountaineering. James Anderson. Nobody had ever called him Jim.

The Doctor read us his thriller, draft by draft. We recognised the enthusiasms, less so the route. But no worry – this was Art, not Science. An interpretation of the Truth.

When it was ready, only the climb's name bothered him. By his own creed, it could no longer be The Solution, for it lacked one. The Apprentice thought hard, leaned across:

'Call it Dissolution,' he said.

Excellent. The Doctor folded his masterpiece and licked the envelope, humming with anticipation. 'It's bound to get in. James Anderson loves this kind of thing. Brisk, factual.'

It did get in.

As a brief note at the end of MISCELLANEOUS:

A correspondent reports a recent rockfall on the NE face of the crag below Meall nan Ceapairean in Coulin. The scar is clearly visible and the surrounding rock unstable. However as the cliff generally is loose, vegetatious and unrewarding at any season, possessing no attractions for climbers, the only danger would seem to be to anyone picnicking directly beneath it.

We thought that shocking. So much for James Anderson. But the Doctor is persistent, faithful to his Faith. A few days later with the help of Evergreen Smith, an expert in these things, he sent his article to *Fresh Air (The HAPPY Outdoor Magazine)*, and the following Thursday told us that the Editor of that publication, passing through Edinburgh, would look him up here at Daddy McKay's (so near the station) between trains that very night.

Sure enough, a short dark-suited tight-moustached character, carrying a briefcase manufactured from the skin of a plastic crocodile and accompanied by a small round-eyed girl child, marched up to our table; shepherded by an anxious Daddy McKay, who endeavoured to hide the sprog behind chairs and the Doctor's raincoat. Introductions.

'Ha, Doctor, glad-to-meecher, name's Brimble, editor, this is Dorothea-me-youngest, up-here-to-see-her-auntie, yes a drink'd go down nice-like, very kind, no not whisky, stick to gin thanks, now' – a deep breath – 'this article is a good article, we'd like it, BUT.' He spread the MS on the table. 'The ending won't DO. Too sudden. Breaks off.'

Our companion protested. 'It's TRUE – that's just what happened; it broke off.' He searched our eyes for affirmation.

'Sorry, won't DO. *Fresh Air* runs Happy Endings to clean, complete, stories. Readers don't want to know what *happened*; they want Happy Endings to clean, complete, stories.' Mr Brimble, an agreeable Cockney-like individual, sipped his gin and lit a small slightly sinister cheroot.

The Doctor blustered. Mr Brimble continued his gin. An uneven battle; for that article had to get in, somewhere.

At this critical point, Dorothea expressed a sudden desire for the Toilet. She grabbed the startled Apprentice: '*You* take me,' she demanded, 'My Dad's busy.' Red-faced, he led her out, hand in hand.

The Doctor argued on. Mr Brimble sipped, understandingly. 'You only have to add a little bit to show you reached the top after all. Just go on from *there*....' He leant over and prodded the MS. A half-inch of ash fell from his cheroot into the Doctor's whisky: our stricken author cried aloud. 'Sorry, Doc, I'll get yer another – Johnny Walker? Black and White?' The Doctor waved an anguished arm at a hastily-summoned Daddy McKay – 'Macallan, Macallan,' he gasped; '16-year-old,' he added. He was becoming unnerved. Brimble was a skilled editor.

Then an irate and buxom wifie burst into the Back Bar, pushing Dorothea (who clutched a bag of crisps donated by the scandalised Daddy McKay) and a scarlet Apprentice before her: 'He's no *fit* to look after a wee lassie, no fit, no fit!' Mirth from the Rugby tables near the door. To them, she poured out the offences: first, he had taken Dorothea absent-mindedly to the Gents', but had met a Gentleman emerging, adjusting his dress, who observed 'Ye cannae tak a lassie in *there*!'; and then, panicking, fled to the Ladies', whence he had been evicted with shrill maledictions by a posse of matrons. 'Tried tae shove himsel intae the Ladies', jist like thaaat...!' 'No fit, no fit at aa!' gleefully chorussed the Rugby tables, loyal to the Rules of the Game.

This was the final straw. Brimble, and his daughter, were skilled editors. Battered by the turmoil and faced with gin, cheroot, crisp-eating child and a choice so obviously Take-it-or-leave-it, the Doctor agreed to continue up the scar by a route neither ourselves nor Gravity had noticed, right to the summit (a feature not unarguably possessed by Meall nan Ceapairean), and then to gaze westward at the golden sun setting over the Magic Celtic Isles (west of Meall nan Ceapairean intervene the midge-breeding magic-denying buttocks of Beinn Damh). And then to Race Down to the lapping sea shore (several miles and two ranges away). 'They all love an ending that Races Down to the lapping sea shore,' confessed Mr Brimble, rising for his train, 'A fine finish to a clean healthy day out of doors.' He belched good-naturedly, and strapped up his plastic crocodile.

Dorothea inflated, and satisfactorily exploded, her crisp packet, showering us with fragments of fry and crystals of salt. We all rose. We all left, the Doctor hurriedly swilling back Macallan and pieces of floating crisp. Ah, well....

None of us mentioned the article again. Two months later it appeared. None of us read it, either (who would buy *Fresh Air*?) But the next Thursday night the Doctor spent the fee (shared with Evergreen Smith, an expert in these things) on several rounds of Knockando, an appropriately-labelled spirit for the climb.

But we shuddered, all the same. How could he, with *his* principles, put his name to an obviously untruthful, Posterity-betraying abomination like that?

'Didn't put my name to it. Used a pen-name.'

What pen-name?

'James Anderson,' he replied.

BEYOND THE LAST BLUE MOUNTAIN

'Exploration is the very soul of the thing....' The Doctor lit his pipe, and stamped his fourth match decidedly after the others into wet heather. 'Even on your Extremes you have to' – puff – '*discover* there aren't any holds.' We were about to add our own contributions to the obvious when we heard a sudden altercation on the slopes below.

It had been a quiet solemn sun-lapped summer evening, the last of our long weekend in the far Northwest. We had fled there for a peace and freedom no longer known in the industrious South – in Lochaber, Mar, Badenoch and other overspoils of leisure, now organised down to the last microchip of bedrock and breakfast. We had come to Coigach simply to explore: hills, cliffs, achingly empty miles of gneiss and lochan – haunts of wild yellow waterlily and roaming sea-otter – beneath blue sky and sailing white cloud. We would enjoy once again the dignity of rarity, without needing to emigrate to that unpeopled paradise of Baffin Land the Doctor so often lectured us about. We carried no mechanical aids to navigation beyond a sealed emergency compass; certainly no Gutter Press of guidebooks; and not one map – we had escaped for three whole days from behind the National Grid.

Marvellous. Our pioneering faculties had been further exercised by continual rain, thick mist and implacable midgery. They registered some success. On the long walk putatively south we had discovered the summit of Cùl Mòr in five places, a recurring excitement only exceeded by our stumbling upon a displaced Atlantic, which – thanks to the cunning of the Apprentice – turned out to taste like Loch Sionnascaig. These delightful uncertainties lost their charm after two and a half days of wet groping, and therefore – as our chief (and eventually sole) enthusiast had tirelessly predicted – we were the more gratifyingly surprised when the weather suddenly turned fine over the last couple of hours.

A glorious prospect of sun, sea and mountain. And where might it be? That beercan glinting in the long low light suggested a popular enough Nature Reserve; that porcupine peak above must surely be Stac Pollaidh; and this tormented No-Man's-Land of a trench tunnelling desperately through the mud in front of us could only be the Tourist Route up it. We had blundered back into the welcoming arms of humanity, on a fine evening. We were content. You could keep your Baffin Land. And the Doctor was about to enjoy his pipe and enlarge upon the – yes, still possible – role of exploration in Scottish mountaineering.

Then this damnable noise below. A knot of struggling people. A fight? Unfortunately, no. They were running towards us, up this appalling morass, a flypaper so entangling them they seemed to be marking time. Fascinated, we watched the plunges forward and the slitherings back. Two-dimensional Purgatory.

The knot unwound into a couple of parties. The larger was led by a hairily-bony middle-aged man in peaty beard and mud-slavering shorts; followed by a diminishing gaggle of – yes – children similarly attired, though beardless. Alongside them, but exhausted and falling back into passive engulfment, wallowed two gesticulating flappers of paper.

The panting string reached us. It seemed unable to stop, and we could only satisfy its breathless entreaties by padding alongside. Most tiresome.

We confirmed species, sex and age, but the ethnic minority as Yorkshire only when the leader, staring devotedly ahead, announced himself as *H*erbert, he came from *H*uddersfield, and he Ran Up *H*igh Mountains – the aspirate adorning this not very illuminating information being blasted forth with every third pounding of his left foot; and those were his *K*ids behind him, real *K*een they were. Nasty little bog-eyed horrors, showering us with mud. Nevertheless, to the point: Herbert swivelled egg-white eyes, gulped out:

'Is this... the way... upStacPollaidh?'

Yes. But it was gey late.

He brandished a wet roll of black paper, and with Olympic agility the Apprentice reached across and grabbed the baton.

We unravelled it and tried to jab out the position, but the juggling and the joggling and the tendency of the exasperated map to part repeatedly at its folds and cast pieces of itself into the morass did not help; though we caught most of them in the slips.

It would have been considerably more convenient to have stopped and discussed the route more soberly, but this was not possible. They must keep going. They were after a Record – a Family Record – and were now enjoying the last few miles of it. Quite possibly they had begun to run at Huddersfield. They were certainly programmed to stop only at the summit of Stac Pollaidh, where a Reception Party was gathered. Herbert should have been in radio communication with it – he waved another baton in his right hand – but mud had ditched the electronics. Yes, of course someone with a radiophone was to have been posted halfway up to guide them, but he had mistaken A837 for A835 and gone up Canisp instead ('Easy enough', gasped Herbert, 'in the mist; you can't *read* those road-signs').

We bellowed our instructions to Keep-On-Up-You-Cannae-Go-Wrong; and any faltering of the father as he cleaned out his nearest ear was greeted by shrieks from the earth-devouring young behind, indistinguishably welded together in each other's wake:

'Go on Dad – Dolly's Blister's Fine!'

Exhausted, we fell back, wiping off micaceous drift and small embedded pebbles that had not enjoyed such a strenuous day since the late Postglacial. We hoped we had imparted sufficient information to get the party up in long enough time for us to vanish before they tried to come down again. We turned in relief; we preferred our own obsessions.

Lord, then we were accosted, belaboured by the other two. Fortunately they had no objections to stopping. They collapsed, purple and stertorous. We hauled them out of the gurgling track on to the heather. We loosened their knotted cagoules and pulled off their bed-rolls and cup-dangling hundredweight of rucksacks; we administered glucose sweets. They resisted a little because we were taking them off the Path, people should stay on the Path....

But they were tough. Hardly had they coughed their breath free of the Pliocene than they were heaving at the octopoid cords of their rucksacks and gouging forth a library of peat-eared and bog-stained volumes. The maps, which we had prised from their hypoglycaemic clench, were shaken out and laid flat. They polished their spectacles and gazed up. Their question followed what by now we recognised as the local oral tradition.

'Is this the way up Stac Pollaidh?'

They explained they had tried to ask Herbert from Huddersfield, but he had been too busy shaking humus out of his stopwatch and they had no breath left to keep up with him. They were glad, really were glad, we had turned up.

'Because this Guidebook', expostulated one, Pete, shaking a coagulated sponge, 'is ALL WRONG....'

'They shouldn't *write* a Guidebook', scolded the other – Cyril – 'if it's ALL WRONG.'

'How could we ever find our way in this kind of place', they chorussed, indicating much of Wester Ross, 'with a Guidebook written ALL WRONG?'

Swift clinical examination by the Doctor diagnosed one specific cause of their complaint – the usual misreading of lefthand bank for true lefthand bank of a crafty little burn. But we agreed it was as difficult to find your way about that particular Guidebook, even when dry, as about a real mountain. At least you had a compass for the mountain.

'Ah, but our compasses have GONE FUNNY.'

The Doctor sighed, and continued his investigation. They possessed no fewer than three compasses (one better than Wull) and had kept them all together waterproof in a tin.... Presumably the consequent wrestle among the respective lines of force had resulted in a common declination to agree – each of the three avoided the others; each preferred its own North. We did not feel competent enough in Lower Physics to explain, still less rectify, this aberration; and advised Pete and Cyril to call it off, Go Down. It was too late, anyway.

Further search among the bookshelves. They extracted a limp and sweating *Hill-Walkers' Handbook*. Rather unnecessarily licking his index finger, Pete flicked for the relevant page. Here it was. Naismith's Formula.... (Ah, Willie, Willie, little did ye reck....)

Cyril produced a folding metre rule. Tongue protruding, he laid a curvilinear length of it across the map and declared the distance to the summit.

The Doctor leant across and moved the rule to the correct mountain. Cyril pointed out the distance was the same, anyway. Pete calculated with his thumb. 'One and a half hours. Easy do it.'

We winced. Although even they could hardly lose their way up a gutter, a gully, a veritable glen such as this path, near the top things opened out and grew teeth, and darkness would close in. It was already six-thirty.

They packed, and hummed to themselves. The Apprentice was all for leaving 'em. 'Plenty of grub, couldn't even climb out of the track, and there'll be a Reception Committee coming down, phones and all. Not our responsibility.' We all wished to flee from such guileless caricatures of our past – maybe indeed of our present – selves. Anyway, wasn't exploration the very soul of the thing?

But our medical companion flinched under the accusing eye of Hippocrates. He tried to resist our dragging him away, he tried to shout a warning over our cheery 'Good Luck, Have a Fine Night'; when two other figures hurtled down that gelatinous groove.

Swiftly as skiers. We leapt back. Cyril and Pete, kneeling at their luggage, stared in amazement.

Squirrch... to a stop. Beside us.

Two unrecognisable objects. Then the glue peeled away, slapped down flatly about them.

Two sodden black balaclavas were pulled off. Two broad muddy paws wiped two broad muddy faces. Two cackling and soil-distributing guffaws.

Geordie and Wull!

Talk of the devil.

'Aye,' said Geordie.

'Aye, aye,' confirmed Wull.

'Terrible day it's been,' declared Geordie.

'Fine the now, though,' pronounced Wull.

Yes, they had been after Bennets, scavenging the guidebook lists as ever. Doing them this time on Mountain Bicycles.

We wondered at such an impure approach from so devotedly conservative a pair.

'O but they're grand things,' said Geordie. 'Tak ye doon in nae time.'

'No so easy gaun up, though,' qualified Wull. Bravely, although draped in two extra tyres, he had only a single bicycle, not being able to carry – or ride – the spare one left behind in the van.

They had enjoyed their day despite this deprivation, and despite the earlier mist and the quite impossible path going up; they had to make, in fact, another track of their own ('Near as bad, mind: thae grippity tyres fair work it aboot....'). They left the bikes below the summit pinnacles, fearing a puncture.

The Doctor took them aside, whispering. These two self-confessed apostates should do our dirty work for us.

They muttered. And then sauntered across to Cyril and Pete, now lifting on each other's packs.

'Ye're no gaun up there the night, like?' growled Geordie, slapping grey alluvium off his lower breeks.

'Wh-why not?'

'Och, its *terrible* up there: aa mist. Ye'd niver get doon alive, that's for sure, lads,' declared Geordie.

'Ye'd be right deid,' acknowledged Wull.

Pete and Cyril complained they could see no mist.

'Of coorse not; no fra *here*. Ye're awfy low doon here; it's when ye get *up* ye see the mist.'

'It's over yon first top,' volunteered Wull.

'There's aye a mist on the true top of Stac Pollaidh, it's near the sea,' explained Geordie. 'Thae ither lads is havin a terrible time – they'll lose the record by hours, ken.'

'An they've freens up there tae help them,' pointed out Wull, 'wi flags an aa; hours an hours,' he added.

'But the map says this top is the summit,' protested Pete, pulling out that indispensable adjunct.

'Let's jist see it.' And Geordie spread it out carefully in the mud, and knelt on it. Wull trod helpfully about its edge.

'Now look – this yin's the *top*; the one ye're *seein* is doon here....' and his uncompromising finger wadged a permanent depression over a now completely unreadable area. 'Yon path, now, doesna go on efter *this*, ken' – another massive prod, with like result. 'An thae lads is stuck *here*' – still more obliteration.

'It's no easy tae find yer way, like, even on a map,' admitted Wull; 'an it gets dark, see, at night....' he further informed them.

'An what's aa this aboot nae compass?' demanded Geordie, rising, shaking most of his B Horizon into the map, folding it brutally up and handing it back to the petrified owners. 'Ye cannae dae things like this in a National Nature Reserve.... It's no like in *England*, ken,' he added, heavy with meaning. Hands on hips, he eyed them severely. Wull shook his head again and again.

Cyril tried to stand his semi-liquid ground. 'Are you the Ranger for here?' he quavered.

Geordie swelled further; his bristling – though mud-encumbered – moustache would have done credit to Inspector McHaig.

'Ah'm no sayin Ah am; Ah'm no sayin ah'm no. Jist *now* Ah'm gien yese Advice, no Orders. Jist awa doon, ma lads, sensible-like – or else... mebbe....' Swell. Bristle. Swell.

They looked at each other, picked up their rucksacks and, without a word, sloppered off down the trough. Silent, heads bent. And safe now from the very soul of the thing.

When they had gone far enough not to return, and we had been told all about gear ratios, tyres, saddles and front and rear suspensions, and about the shrill festivities cape-capering in Record Time about the embarrassed cairn above, Geordie and Wull donned balaclavas again; they thrust legs over their dripping steeds, stood up on the pedals, and squeezed off.

'We'll be doon afore ye!' Geordie bawled back.

'Get there first, like!' shouted Wull through orbiting spare tyres. 'Heh, heh, heh!'

We watched them gather speed until, when the wheels locked solid with glaur, they took off from the steep parts with a terrifying *schuss*, like toboggans; leaving behind twin ditches worthy of the Forestry Commission.

Far out of sight, with triumphant hoots and ringing of bells.

From equally far above came cheers and clapping, a sing-song, bangs of fireworks and thunderflashes.

We went down through the last of the glorious evening – sea, mountain and loch – blind to it all, heads together, planning our three weeks in Baffin Land.

The Doctor knew of a good guidebook to it.

BEATING THE RECESSION

It was a fine late-October day, in the middle of well, either Gaick or the Monadhliaths, we are not supposed to say which. We strode over snow-freckled heather, across a plateau of bowed heads similarly dusted. Between them, huge declivities of black glens. Above us, the cold blue sky of early winter.

We always came here at this time, to breathe the change of air and tread freshly frosted earth. Soon all over Scotland the gullies would be in condition, the faces beckoning with ice. A glittering prospect. It should be a good winter. Why, there was even a fair stretch of snow already in the little corrie just below us.

We ran down to it. Just to get that hard slither beneath our heels again.

It was snow right enough, an inch or two on top of old hard stuff. Really old snow, dirty, scattered with bits of twig and spruce needles. Spruce needles! Here in the middle of the treeless plateau of – er – Gaick. 'Up-draughts,' explained the Doctor. But he could not explain the *depth* of old snow, at this time of year. Nor – look – the spoor of tracked vehicles across it. We kicked – hard as ice. The Doctor screwed in his axe (he'd brought one, to make things look wintry); but couldn't reach bottom. Last season's? Not possible, these warm years, at just under 3000 feet. But, still, the corrie faced north-east and could catch miles of blown snow from every direction on this table-land.

Then we saw snow fences, to gather drifts and encourage them into the corrie. And machinery – a snow-maker with its hose snaking into a plastic lochan, and a couple of piste-bashers, pistie-beasties. And coloured sticks marking the slalom course. Obviously a good snow reservoir like this had been taken over by the Ski Industry.

Yes, a track led up from below. With a truck, tractors and a bull-dozer. And workmen. And buildings down there, and a cable over pylons – clearly, restaurants and chair-lifts....

We hurried over. The Doctor was astonished. 'No mention of skiing here in any plans I've seen. The main road, yes; not here. Must find out!'

The truck and bogeys were being loaded with great heaps of stuff cleared off the snow, and taking them down the roadway.

Heaps... of spruce branches! Spruce branches...?

Ecological snow fencing? Why taking them away,then? We went up to the gaffer and enquired. Pure nosiness, of course. He smiled slowly.

'We're jist makkin ready for the winter. Now the hard weather's settin in. Clearin awa the cover.' And would not be drawn further. 'Na, ye'll hae to ask Dr MacPherson. It's his affair.'

A bell rang under the Doctor's fishing hat. 'Archie MacPherson?' he asked.

'Some might call him Erchie,' was the experienced reply. 'But he's owre there,' pointing.

The Doctor peered. 'It is, it is old Archie. Lord, I knew he was back, what a coincidence. Fancy *him* starting a Ski Resort. In an Economic Recession, too. Let's go and ask him about it.'

On the way he explained that Archie, a fellow-student of his, though older and studying geology, had gone abroad and struck it lucky with oil in Alaska. Had made a fortune. A prudent man, hard-headed, very reserved. In fact, downright Mean, yet possessing a fairly mineralogical sense of humour. He'd retired early, come back a few years ago and bought an estate in the old MacPherson country. A sentimentalist, like all these self-made men. A hell of a lot of land, the Doctor recalled, here in (shall we say) Gaick. 'So that's what he's up to. Ski resorting – strange; he never used to *like* people.'

Archie MacPherson, a short powerful pipesmoking man in an old cap and filthy raincoat, did not seem to like us, at any rate. He grimly surveyed the Doctor, and ignored the Apprentice and myself. But we overheard.

Yes, this was his estate. Then a pipe-smoking silence.

The Doctor, avoiding the main question, chose to ask: 'Spruce branches...?'

'From my woods in the glen.'

Yes, but why moving 'em down again?

'Because I brought them up here in the summer.' Stare, puff.

The Doctor, pipeless and thus at a disadvantage, could only venture further in pure nosiness. 'Why bring them up in the first place?'

MacPherson looked him over, then examined us carefully. We stepped back. The Doctor began to re-introduce us but the pipe waved him down. We had, however, passed scrutiny. The pipe answered.

'To preserve the snow. I am building up snow here, year after year. This corrie collects a great amount, I bring in a lot more, and it's sheltered from any warm wind. The branches keep off the sun. Give insulation. We get very little thaw even in a hot summer; even after a poor winter.'

So things became clearer. It *was* for skiing. Year after year, and we'd never heard of it. Archie had bad P.R. But a wonderful idea, trying to keep last season's snow to gain an early start to this one. We asked the direct question, indirectly:

'You're certainly making a fine place here for skiing in the winter. It should become very popular.'

He withered us. Skiing? Skiing!

'Do you think I've nothing better to think about than... Skiing! Nothing better to spend my time and money on than a childish self-indulgence like that?' He put away his pipe. His eyes became dreamy. 'I suppose you've heard how they've managed to bring back ospreys? And sea eagles? And reindeer? And how some people – good luck to them – want to bring back bears and wolves? A kind of palaeo-conservation mania, for reintroducing the Post-Glacial fauna?' We nodded, quite at sea (was he going to suggest Polar Bears?).

'Well, *I* am bringing back – a GLACIER. I am reintroducing a Late-Glacial inhabitant. I *have* brought back a glacier, the beginnings of one, and here I am *conserving* it. I know something about glaciers, I worked with them long enough in Canada and Alaska. *This*', he stamped vigorously on the snow, 'is a glacier. Now' – he stared fixedly at us – 'I am being confidential, I don't want it blabbed around, encouraging' – he stared at us one by one – 'fools here to poke and prod and break up the surface. The first few years of a glacier's life are critical. Disturbed, it never develops, fades away. Mind you, once settled in, it makes its own climate, doesn't need cosseting like this' – he waved at truck and tractors – 'keeps on growing, cooling things down. Positive feedback.' He took out his pipe again, a little warmed by our astonishment. He struck matches, the flames quivered.

He was fiercely possessive of his glacier. Any suggestion that it might merely be an occasionally perennial snowfield like that in Garbh Choire Mòr provoked wrath. He flung the last match away.

'I've piled enough depth now for the bottom to be pressed to ice. It's begun to FLOW. A whole metre forward this last year – look how those sticks have moved. Internal strains developing too – subsurface cracks and incipient crevasses – found 'em by sonics and lasers. Yes, it's a glacier right enough – though for Final Popular Proof', he added scornfully, 'we'll need OPEN crevasses, I suppose.' He glared at us.

Alas, we failed to disguise our doubts sufficiently. He plucked out his pipe, spun round, waved dismissively and marched off to a rusty Land Rover. So much for the hospitality of an old friend.

'A hard man, Archie, a difficult man,' observed the Doctor, lighting up now the competition had gone. 'But a wonderful depth of cold compressed motivation. He'd wear down any opposition. Just keeps pressing on.'

We strolled over his acre or so of proto-glacier. If only it *were* a glacier; the first for 8000-odd years. We began to thrill. One man alone, fighting Global Warming. Reconstituting his own glacier. A world-wide recession of them, but not here. Private enterprise indeed.

We inspected the outfall, a mini-snout, its progress being measured weekly with the latest apparatus by that dour-faced Archie, kneeling in the patched-up breeks of a visionary millionaire. Soon, perhaps it would spill over and down the burnside, through the old gap its predecessor had made, re-enter its rightful glen, grunting and shoving aside with piggy delight turf and trees, piling up boulders, heaving itself into great blue and white icefalls between scoured cliffs – making wonderful climbing.... It would chill all its fellows into resurrection: the A9 would run a gauntlet, fanged and grinning above you. And here we were at the *start* of all this!

We sighed and gazed around at the resolutely unglaciated landscape.

Ah, well. Then – a *crack*. The Apprentice had disappeared. He was not there when we turned in alarm. Just a hole. And a furious voice from below.

He had fallen through the crust. Was jammed about five feet down in a baby dimple that hugged him lovingly – and our rucksack and spare line.

'A real crev...' gasped the Doctor, stepping back: and vanishing likewise.

I made for the side and sank slowly; my last view was of a couple of grinning tractor men and a grimly complacent pipe.

We were cold down there in the pale blue; damnably cold. But we needn't do a Joe Simpson: it was an infant catastrophe, the glacier was just learning: not deep – we were all unhurt and loudly demanding a rope.

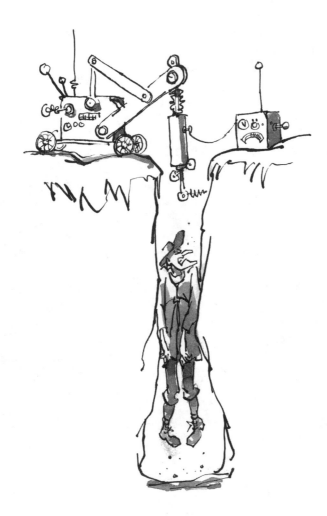

Archie took his time. He needed photographic proof, he explained, and samples of the failed crust before it was messed up by things like rescue operations. Great probes and instruments with winking lights purred about us unfeelingly, intent on their personal business. Things like huge dentists' drills – quite on their own – operated small toothy saws, trepanning the ice alarmingly near our immobilised heads. We supposed it was really very necessary – after all, this glacier was on a Life Support System.

Eventually, all was completed and they decided to haul us out – by floodlight. We stood grey, frozen and shivering on the heather as the men jovially slapped back our circulation. We stared at the equipment still trundling up and down the cables from the laboratories twinkling below. Like a dream. We were speechless. And Archie?

Archie was as pleased as ever he allowed himself to be. As pleased as if he'd reintroduced bears and they'd eaten someone. His glacier felt at home, had asserted its place in the Late-Glacial biosphere. He twinkled icily beneath the stars. He crackled orders. Cameras still flashed: holes, footsteps and broken-up surface were recorded.

Archie in fact exuded a kind of Polar bonhomie. Although we had messed up his – Scotland's – glacier inexcusably, we *had* provided Final Popular Proof, and our hungry (and thirsty) expectations rose, not to mention hopes of a roaring wood fire.

Yes, he had thawed; he took us down in the Land Rover, the gaffer driving, and remarked how cold and hungry we must be.

Ah! – we stopped at the Big House (dark and shuttered). Archie got out. 'You'll be mighty glad, I'm sure, of a good meal right now.' Splendid man! We agreed heartily and half-rose in our seats. 'Now they do a fine one at a little place in Dalwhinnie,' he went on, describing a ghastly refrigerator we'd suffered in before, 'It's rather late, but just mention my name and they'll likely open for you. It's quite cheap, too. Well; good to have met you. And thanks for the Subsurface Monitoring,' he added. 'Quite useful, in fact.' Slammed the door, waved, and went.

The gaffer dropped us at the car. He seemed damnably amused about something. We climbed stiffly into cold seats.

'A hard man, Archie,' the Doctor reaffirmed, as we drove off to pie, chips and a gas fire at Pitlochry, 'Mean as hell: but if anyone can encourage a glacier, it's him....'

WITCH'S SABBATH

It was a most extraordinary chain of coincidences. It began, like much else, in the back bar of Daddy McKay's. After that first extraordinary coincidence, others followed, as the Doctor said, 'Exponentially, like Evolution.' Yet – like Evolution – no more (of course) than a series of quite random occurrences; born of climate, topography and our by then disordered imagination. No Malicious Intent behind it. None whatever. We are quite sure now. But we are still careful where we go at that time of year.

We had been studying the map at our table by the fire. We had settled Saturday's campsite high in Coire ____ : no, I shall not name it, nobody shall be lured there – and we sat back. The Doctor called for another round, put away his spectacles and lit his pipe. Peace. Puff. We gazed about us. The other end of the room was a scrummage of Rugby overflows from the front bar. Some kind of pre-season Border Sevens reunion. Thumpings and singing.

Our whiskies arrived, were set out, and the Doctor – as so often – had paid and was stuffing his wallet in the back of his breeks when a voice from above exclaimed:

'So ye're gaun tae Coire ____ ?'

A great square forefinger, of good eye-gouging elasticity, stubbed down on our map, bang on the campsite. We looked up, astonished.

The voice belonged – just – to a huge barn-shouldered, micro-eared, screw-nosed individual clutching unsteadily a fistful of foam. It continued, much awash.

'Ah've been there as well. Ah've climbed on thae cliffs. When Ah wis climbin, ken. KEN?'

We smiled indulgently; but had hoped for virgin ground....

'Niver again. Pit me aff climbin fer guid.'

We raised eyebrows. They rose still further when, with much elliptical swaying about us, our informant explained they tried one good line for two whole days.

' – An couldna make it!' His orbit was fairly regular and through a sort of Doppler effect we gathered that everything had gone wrong on that climb. Stonefall, stonefall – aye, *up* as well as down.

'Ah cannae tell ye the hauf o whit went on.' Anyway, they did not succeed. But they gave the climb a name, nevertheless.

'We did that. We caad it' – screwing his eyes – '...*Poltergeist!*'

This last, most unexpected, word was delivered with remarkable skill, considering his condition; though the sibilant bespattered our map. The Doctor hastily wiped and refolded it, but our visitor, relaxing his concentration, lurched heavily and drenched him with Eighty Shilling Ale or suchlike. Some contaminated the whisky, and a dollop landed in his pipe. Steam, bubbling, indignation.

Answering ribald summonses from his own table, our acquaintance staggered away, finding time and equilibrium to pause and bellow back:

'It's no a right place at aa!'

Though not as put out as the Doctor's pipe, we were taken aback.

'At least, they didn't climb anything – we should make some brand-new routes,' the Doctor reassured us, swabbing his bowl with a strip of *Evening News*. 'But what a remarkable coincidence his being here tonight.' The first, alas, of many, as I have suggested.

Before we managed up, several Saturdays had passed, and soothed apprehensions. The low sun gilded luminous late October colours; a good season for Coire _____ which, unusually, was neither stalked nor forested. We had glimpsed its unrecorded crags from a neighbouring hill that summer.

A grassy track led there, and we parked at its beginning, by an ancient cottage. We knocked at the door.

No answer.

Then an old woman appeared on the road behind, lugging a large black plastic bag.

'That'll be her – been out for messages,' cried the Doctor. The Apprentice ran to help with the bag. His knees buckled under it. We stepped aside.

She opened the door. The Apprentice relinquished his burden, like a ton of rocks. A cat emerged from within and rubbed against the old girl's rumpled black stockings. The Doctor offered a conciliatory finger; but hastily withdrew as the creature arched back and spat eyes.

The old lady cackled. Her own eyes were black diamonds, dramatically crossed. It was difficult to look at her. Occasionally both eyes agreed to stare at you together, and this was even more off-putting. A regular witch.

We hoped our car would not be in the way.

'Na, na.'

We explained where we were going, what we hoped to do.

She cackled again, booted the cat indoors, effortlessly lifted the bag and fixed us with sudden binocular vision.

'Yon's no a place to go campin in.'

Shook head, went inside, snibbed the door. That was that.

'Funny old girl. But to everyone here, mountains are dangerous,' smiled the Doctor, magnanimously.

We splashed up the track, the Apprentice rubbing his biceps – 'Almost half a bloody hundredweight, those messages. Tough old bird. Must have got a bus, or a hitch.' The nearest shop was unimaginable miles away, the last bus in 1953. 'Broomstick,' explained the Doctor.

We camped in the Coire, on its only bit of green, bisected by a burn and facing grey soaring cliffs. A perfect evening, long clear shadows, midgeless. After pitching the tent we wandered up to look. One line was immediately evident, a rib, the only unbroken route. Like all such crags, distance lent the sole enchantment (or so we thought...). The rib was hardly even sporting, but should at least be virgin.

Which reminded us of the curious episode at Daddy McKay's. We laughed, maybe over-heartily; for dusk was falling; and raced down to the tent.

The Doctor halted, puzzled.

'Lord, it's the other side of the burn. Don't remember crossing any water.'

None of us did. But there it stood, neatly pitched, primus outside, just as we'd left it. Both banks of the burn looked identical. Easy to mistake. But we *did* think.... No matter. These things happen.

The Apprentice and I laid out bags and the Doctor began cooking. The primus refused to light. Several times. Such a reliable one, too. Moreover, both prickers snapped their whiskers. Odd. He swore continuously, in frustration.

Rain arrived. But even inside, the stove withstood oaths and entreaties. We supped on bread and cold spam, drank cold burn water. Everything was cold. We pulled bags up to shoulders and sipped the Doctor's whisky, perhaps too often. (He had resisted offering it to the primus – 'One can go too far.')

But his pipe, even, would not light. The bowl was soaked, the water-proof pouch was soaked; and now the remaining matches had dissolved to paste. The Doctor's jaw dropped at this chain of disasters.

'Well, I'm damned!'

The response to this unwise assertion, or admission, was remarkably prompt. A fearsome flash through the fabric; and an emphatic disapprobation of thunder, rock to rock, summit to summit. Our headlamp went out. Rain pelted.

In the suitably Faustian silence and dark that followed, we remained speechless.

'Mains fused,' remarked the Doctor at last, wearily. He retired beneath his bag. We did likewise. Sometimes, ye cannae win.

We were physically uncomfortable, also. A sharp stone jabbed my shoulder-blades wherever I lay, although we had tooth-combed the turf before pitching. But we must have slept, for we were woken several times. Once by a thing, or things, trampling about outside. 'Sheep,' mumbled the Doctor. Guys twanged. Heavy breathing. Stomp, stomp, twang. The Apprentice, wroth, shone his torch through the door.

Nothing, of course, there. 'We've frightened it off, anyway.' Then *his* light went out. Just as well, for the sudden illumination of a horny head, however placidly ruminant, might have upset us by then. Trying to replace the bulb with a spare, the Apprentice lost both. He sank back, beyond care. Then yelped. Something was poking his back. I felt beneath me. He had got my stone. 'Continental drift,' yawned the Doctor, as he turned over.

At first rim of dawn I woke to distant music and singing. I crawled out: a cool clear half-light, untenanted. My disturbed companions were not enthralled by the serenade. 'That old wifie's radio', growled the Apprentice, 'coming up on the wind.' The Doctor favoured burn water across pebbles. 'Often heard it like that. Mass in D Major, MacGregor's Lament, Hibs *versus* Hearts. Or it could be some ramshammy in that fairy mound by the track.'

We did not sleep any more. While the Apprentice tried blowing the kiss of life into the primus, from matches dried in his hair, we re-told odd happenings we'd met elsewhere in the Magic West. The Doctor sucked his empty pipe and recounted the jumping about of tables and chairs in two houses in North Uist, and the minister's importing a Priest from the southern island to tranquillize them – Rome enjoying closer relations with the Devil; no, *he* hadn't been at that particular country dance, but his friend, his friend certainly had. Interruptedly – for my stone had returned – I described footsteps up and down the stairs at Steall Hut; which the Doctor explained as a tap dripping. The Apprentice remembered a fairy – 'fine-looking girl, a bit thin, but smashing legs' – he'd encountered by the loch at Quinag; when he'd grabbed his camera, she'd gone. 'Just as well for you,' remarked the Doctor, warned by the misadventures in 1692 of the Rev. Robert Kirk, M.A. 'Did she have wings? If so, she wasn't local; our fairies don't have wings. She'd be an English visitor, flown up.' The Apprentice confessed it wasn't wings he'd been thinking about just then.

After a cold breakfast we set off for the crag, meticulously checking rope and the little equipment we thought necessary. 'Bring a few pegs: they don't like iron,' advised the Doctor. His jocularity jarred at that hour.

We found no other excuse for pitons. The route was at most a V.D. and surprisingly sound. But mist thickened, and stones – as our beery prophet had foretold – began to trickle down the gullies either side; fortunately still obeying the laws of gravity.

Then, out of the mist above, a cackling; like the old wifie's, but harder, as of bones rattling. 'Tough old bird,' quoted the Doctor, with mirth, but notably studious of his holds. A fearful yell; followed by stones and earth, and a great beating of air. Mouths dried. Our leader paused.

A black shape above. Flat head, great beak. Huge wings. Flap, flap. Cackle. Rattle.

'A bloody raven,' gasped the relieved Apprentice, 'Gerrout, you ___!' He flung bits of mountain. 'Careful,' cried the Doctor....

Words were lost in a sudden wind that roared up – yes, up – the gullies, carrying grass, heather, sand and small stones. Anoraks billowed about our heads, we were belted hard on the backside by pebbles; they ricochetted about us – we drew hoods tight. Rain followed. The raven guffawed.

'Up-draught: atmospherics,' bellowed the Doctor above the din. 'We're near the top, anyway,' and he decamped hurriedly to the left. Still roped – no precautions seemed excessive that day – we scrambled towards the summit, the Apprentice clutching, I noticed, a piton with religious fervour.

We never found the top in the mist. Our compass shared the atmospheric excitement; it cavorted like Uist furniture. We gained a distinct impression of not being at all wanted; and descended the east rim of the corrie into comparative shelter and considerable relief. As we coiled our rope, the Doctor was explaining how the configuration of Coire ____ must inevitably provoke such Aeolian excesses. 'No wonder those chaps called it Pol....' We all stopped.

But the three great ghostly shapes now blooming in the mist evoked no more response.

'Brocken Spectres,' sighed the Doctor. He waved an exhausted arm.

A spectral arm was raised in reply. 'Of course, that's what the Grey Man of MacDhui is,' he added, restored by demonstration, 'Curious how both Collie *and* Kellas – a much more reliable chap – got all het up and fled. Just atmos...

At this point the third Spectre, which was myself, raised its arm. Unfortunately, I had both mine folded in front of me. Then they all, with waving limbs, billowed towards us.

'Atmos...pherics,' gasped the Doctor as we belted down, leaping rocks, galloping bogs. I glanced back. The three Spectres had been replaced by a large Dog bounding after us. It was gaining, we felt its breath, heard its thump of paws, a long howl.... I remember crying 'Help!' and the hoarse croaks of my companions were no less urgent.

Then suddenly we burst into sunlight, and into an astonished couple of walkers on the track.

They were elderly, respectable, tweed- and green-jacketed, and most taken aback. We stumbled to a halt, sobbing and gasping, the Apprentice mouthing 'Dog, dog,' as he tripped over a tussock and literally fell into the arms of the lady.

'There, there,' she said, holding him up, 'you shouldn't be so upset. He's quite harmless; a *dear*, really. Jeremy, Jeremy,' she called. A black Labrador panted up and jumped about and licked the unhappy purple-faced Apprentice. 'Look, he's making friends. Jeremy, what *have* you been doing to frighten this poor young man?'

They were very kind. We parted with thanks, and feeble explanations. To reassemble himself, the Doctor extolled to us the smart rainproof jacket of the pink old gentleman – who was the very picture of some retired General or Brigadier. 'Grenfell – the sort of cloth you could buy before the war; wears for ever, not like this terylene trash. Wonder how he gets it nowadays?' But we had been shaken.

During our limp back to camp, the Doctor valiantly attributed everything to Atmospherics: wind and mist. 'But a hell of a fright', he admitted, 'at the time.' We could no longer throw stones (throw stones!) at Collie and Kellas.

When we reached the site, no tent. But there it was – on the other side of the burn again. We said nothing. Atmospherics. Packing up, the Apprentice and I searched for our wandering stone. The turf proved innocent, everywhere. We decided to forget that, too.

Just before the car, a sudden owl terrified us. Then the Doctor knocked on the cottage door, to thank the old wifie. No reply. Utter desertion. 'Gone shopping for another half-hundredweight of porridge oats,' muttered the Apprentice, heaving his rucksack into the boot.

Coire _____ had not quite finished with us. The old Mercedes itself was bewitched. It would not start. The Doctor fumbled under the bonnet. Unwisely he had left the key switched on and the gear in, and must have touched some nerve, for with a roar the great beast leapt into the ditch.

The crofter who eventually – he lived two miles away and it was the Sabbath – tractored us out was not forthcoming about Coire _____ , and we did not press him. We asked him, though, to convey our thanks to the old lady who, we explained, was not in.

'Effie MacFarlane? The Cailleach Dhubh? She's no been in these three month, she's with her son ten mile this side o Inverness.' We blenched. 'But, yess, he has been visiting his daughter down there at the hotel some Saturdays, mebbe he wass giving her a lift up for the day.' We brightened. 'Or mebbe not: she's no very *communicative*; and mebbe jist as well....' he added, darkly.

The Doctor delicately proffered recompense for the tow-out. Our rescuer restarted his engine. 'No, no, I would not be doing it at *all* on a day such as this', (it was, you'll remember, the Sabbath) 'but for a traveller in distress.' He leant down and eyed us keenly. 'But what were you *doing* up there in the Coire, on a day such as this? It wass not for *pleesure?*'

'No, no,' we fervently assured him. 'Examining rocks,' volunteered the Doctor.

'Geologists, mebbe?'

We did not disagree. 'Business, well, business is no perhaps the same as pleesure on a day such as this: but, yess, it iss a dangerous place, Coire ——, a very dangerous place.'

'Oh, not if you're used to doing what we do,' laughed the Doctor. 'Geologising,' he added hastily.

The crofter stopped his engine, turned sideways in his seat, laid his hands on his knees and gazed down seriously upon us.

'It wass before the war, it wass this time of year, it wass this day of the week, there wass two people from the hotel went up this very track to the Coire, a colonel or general it wass, and his lady. And' – pause – 'they never came back.'

'Never came back?' We thought of hotel bills and Captain Rawlings' prudent decampment at Balqueenie.

'Never came back.' The crofter raised his head and stared into distance. 'There iss rocks and bogs up there, and there wass search parties for weeks but – nothing wass found.'

'So they've not been seen since,' said the Doctor, amused; 'Very sad.'

'Oh, they have been *seen* often enough.' The crofter laughed, and our flesh began to creep. 'That iss the trouble. All three of them.'

'Three?'

'Yess; they had a dog.' Our flesh crept further; as far, in fact, as it could.

'A... a black dog?'

'Very likely a black dog. People have heard it *howling.*'

'Did the gentleman have a white moustache?' croaked the Doctor.

'Very likely a white moustache, but: *I* do not know. *I* have not seen them myself. *I* do not go up there. It iss a dangerous place. Especially on a day such as this.'

He swung round and restarted the engine.

'What was the dog's name?' shouted the Doctor, hoarsely.

'I do not know.' He slipped into gear, he leant down to us as he

jerked off. It may have been a smile, or concentration on his clutch –
'But Effie would know. *She* would be knowing.'

He saluted gravely and puttered away in blue smoke.

No one wished to speak first. The Doctor, after thinking, no doubt,
about pre-war Grenfell cloth, announced briskly: 'We can't stand here,
it's getting dark. Jeremy and his friends may come back this way, they
may take the long way round to the hotel – or they may not come back.
It's no concern of ours. Dozens of generals at the hotel, I dare say. More
than enough to make up any – er – deficiency.' We saw his point, and
climbed in.

'Probably,' he declared, driving off and reaching out to wipe the last
of the ditch from the windscreen, 'in fact, certainly, it's all very simple.
A chain of coincidences; extraordinary, but nothing more – blast!!'

A cat, a black cat, *the* cat, had leapt from the dyke and under our
front wheels. There was a bang and a bump. We stopped and jumped
out. Of all the...

Yet, there was no cat. Or pieces of cat. Only the song of birds – not
owls – the gentle autumn breeze, the bliss of early evening about us.
Coire _____ smiled grimly in its shadow.

We were relieved. 'A wee innocent beastie,' burbled the Apprentice,
demoralised, or moralised, by the day. He was cut short by violent
oaths from the Doctor.

'Flat, bloody flat. The front tyre's burst. Burst. And a new one last
week. At *that* price....'

We arrived home very late. There had been a further coincidence or
two. Almost an hour later, just before Inverness, a crowd. Torches. We
stopped. Police. 'A doctor here?' He jumped out, disappeared. We ate
crisps.

Ambulance, lights flashing. Amid thanks and handclasps, he climbed
in again.

'What was it?'

He appeared lost in thought. 'An old lady. Knocked down by a car
about an hour ago – about when we ran over the cat.... Just found. Only
broke an ankle. She'll get over it.' He turned round to us – at 60 m.p.h.
on the Kessock bridge – and gleamed.

'She's a tough old bird.'

No, he did not ask Effie if she'd been up the day before. No, he did not ask the dog's name. No, he did not even ask if she *was* Effie. It was dark and we'd all had enough for one weekend. And no, we never enquired further. Corries can be dangerous places, and West Highlanders, particularly on the Sabbath, can display a black sense of humour. Let it remain a tale to be told by torchlight, like the Steall staircase, the mobile homes of Uist, the Apprentice's fairy. Or – wherever should we be?

However, one last coincidence. No bad thing to be late, the Doctor assured us. His wife had given the neighbours' children a Party the night before, it would have taken till now to clean up, it had been a 'Do you know,' (here he turned round again, at 80 m.p.h. on that dreadful Dalwhinnie straight) ' – a Hallowe'en Party'.

So there was a rational explanation, after all.

JUST OVER 20

This tale is an Extra. Tagged on. Like what it describes.

Now, we are wary of Beginners. They usually End by embarrassing us. Especially the young ones, whom you can't curse satisfactorily. Previous examples will doubtless be recalled.

We therefore uncooperatively resist requests to Take Up Youngsters Who Are Interested. Having been so often Let Down.

However, last spring we were persuaded, by no less experienced a practitioner at the Bar than Daddy McKay, to take an example of new blood (as he put it) up with us the next Sunday on some easy snow-plod. The weather was forecast fine. Daddy himself was, of course, obliging a friend (they always are) and didn't know the applicant (they never do). We pointedly refused – even after so many Thursday nights of his discreet ethanolic dispensations – to oblige our Host, if the victim he allotted us was juvenile. So Daddy got on to the phone behind the bottles. Through a foam of clatter, gurgle and banging we were assured that no self-satisfied adolescent or infant prodigy was involved.

Indeed, Daddy called across to us: 'Seems to be 20 at least!' Then, to his phone, 'What, just over 20?'; to us again, '21 by Sunday, in fact! That's enough, eh? That should satisfy you!' 'What sex?' the Apprentice bawled back, becoming more interested. But the noise was frightful. Daddy waggled the phone, shook his head, and put it down. He forced his way over to us. 'Line's terrible. Can't tell you just now – you'll have to find out on Sunday....' A little joke; he smiled and rubbed his hands.

What could we do? Refusal would deeply disappoint. Just after his (or her) birthday, too. That weekend, then, we awaited our Fourth Person in the car park below Lochnagar. The name of this lamb who was to look out for us was – improbably – Smith. Francis (or -es) Smith. We kept to the outside of the burgeoning throng, and tried to look as like ourselves as we could.

Then a car drove up, perilously close, and a figure jumped out and clasped our hands damply. We flinched. Our fears were confirmed. Male, enthusiastic; but, at least, certainly over 20. 'Yes, Smith's the

name.' He blinked eagerly at us in turn. 'Francis Smith?' 'No, Freddie....'
Ah, some misunderstanding on the phone. That noise! No, no, Frankie
would be here in a moment....

Fr... Two of 'em? The other figure climbed out, a plump and accosting
character. Frankie Smith. We submitted, numbly.

Another car sloshed up. Five people, of both sexes – or, rather, of
either sex, or each sex – you know what I mean, leapt out, in eye-
splitting anoraks and – were introduced. 'So good of you.'

'But Mr McKay said.... We thought....' The Doctor spluttered;
helpless. The Smiths and others regarded us kindly. Then a minibus
drew alongside, tooted, and a whole mob tumbled out of its rustily
sliding doors....

An F. Smith began introductions. We cut him short. We began to
count. It began to dawn. Just over 20. Not years. People. Just over 20
people.... 21, in fact; this Sunday.

It was no use. We couldn't disappoint them. And, true, there were no
sprogs or suspicions of sprogs. It seemed (so far) good weather and
they were all so excited. Being assured no more would arrive, we
checked their boots and clothes – adequate. Axes... none. So we
shouldered all our full-lengths of rope and moved the expedition on to
the hill.

The snow was spring and the trail well broken. Axes not needed, for
once. The Doctor stalked in front, the Apprentice and I shepherded the
rear, for any byes. We answered questions. We smiled at jokes. We
were almost looking forward to remembering this trip. We were (almost)
remembering our own first mountain; almost remembering not
to be ashamed at having enjoyed that wonderful far-off day.

We reached the Top, as promised. Together with a few score others.
We identified, excusably rashly, all the peaks that became visible when
people chanced to move out of the way. But they (the peaks) were
vanishing one by one. Clouds had gathered and were lowering. *Splat*;
splat. The usual late spring blizzard was developing. A thrill ran through
our receptive charges. Real Excitement.

We acted promptly. Strung 'em all together on our combined ropes.
It was not easy, for similar garlands were being assembled around us.
Dozens of play groups. Like DNA.

Then the storm broke. We plunged off, the Doctor exuberantly gallant ahead, brandishing his axe, the Apprentice appropriately stern at the rear; myself, unroped, patrolling the flanks.

It was easy enough. The tracks were unmissable, even in the few metres' visibility. And all were tied on, nose to tail; no chance of any getting lost. I counted them several times, to make sure; the average came to 20.8 – statistically comforting. Someone, probably, was not quite all there; but several had looked that way, anyhow. The advantages of such a long string became evident: one end was always above, or below, any dubious stretch of topography, and could fairly accurately wag the rest of the dog back on to course. It was a doddle, and we felt rather pleased with ourselves. Our charges, naturally, were delighted, and kept stopping to tell me so, seriously discomposing those tied on to them before and behind. A shunting progress that frequently derailed the Doctor and finally uncoupled the Apprentice.

Just above the car park we left the cloud and, because bellies and backsides were understandably chafed by then, untied the kilometres of rope. We repeatedly counted the liberated: 23, 18, 26; but some had gambolled off, and so many passing goats had joined us, we hadn't the heart to persevere.

We shooed 'em down over simple slopes to the car park, and once there tried to sort them into the cars and the minibus. The motorists were easy enough in theory, for they were supposed to know each other, according to the Messrs Smith; but the minibus held a job lot of Rent-A-Ramble and Wish-A-Walk, who were too delighted with having gone up – and come down – to think about much else. So we had to try and line everybody up and count in real earnest.

This became difficult. Buses and cars roared and flashed, spun and smoked beside – between – us. Weather blasted across us. Other groups splashed through us, or adhered like glue; or bore away some of our own. Brownian Motion. We flew about and swore. The Doctor recalled (much later) the Magic Pigs of Cruachu, that no man could ever count – *when they were being numbered they would not stay; if anyone tried to number them, they would be gone....* We plunged as low as 14 at one time, and shook with apprehension; then the Apprentice pointed out that those from the cars were inside them, eating pieces. And once soared up to a giddy 36, when the Balloch and Dumbarton Girl Guides' Outdoor Activities included latching on to our left-hand end. One of the F.

Smiths gave us a list of names, but as the top half had dissolved away, that was of little help (we did notice yet another Smith, F.).

Eventually the cars were satisfied and rolled off, bearing their seven. Now for the minibus. Every seat had to be occupied – the ultimate check. It was a hell of a job to get the jabbering sleet-dripping figures, vigorously changing clothes and shouting with mirth, to sit down for one moment; and then you usually included the driver or the anxiously bobbing Doctor by mistake. One old girl was lustily singing, with the voice of two, *The Back o Bennachie*. Fourteen. 14 plus 7 equals 21. At last.... We let them drive off. In the opposite direction to that much-serenaded mountain: home to Edinburgh.

Phew.... Never again, as so often said. Lucky this time, but.... Then: a long too-bright youth pushed up to us, wiping his sweaty prow.

'This Frankie Smith's lot? Fraid I'm late.'

We clutched him savagely. Where had he been? Been? Up Eagle Buttress, with some friends he'd seen as soon as he came off the bus that morning. Had a real good time. Fab. Was lent a pick, crampons, helmet an all. Better than a bloody snowplod, eh? And he laughed like granite and demanded his seat.

But we had counted (more or less) 21 on the rope and despatched 21 certainly off in the various vehicles....

Then a commotion behind us. Pitfoulie MRT; with its new fluorescently-plumaged (Discovery) Land Rover. Someone was missing. Had not come down. Couldn't be found at her bus.

Ignoring the indignation of our belated proselyte, we squeezed towards a bereaved minibus, stark with a vacant seat. Eck, the Pitfoulie leader, was thoughtfully sucking his pencil before a gesticulating driver; his radiophone squawked in the slush at his feet.

The Doctor sized things up. An Aberdeen minibus. Lots of real old weatherproof crumblies inside, aghast or asleep.

He grabbed the driver.

'Was she a big fat wifie in blue? Fond of singing?' ....